W9-ANG-283

THE BASIC
GUIDE TO SEWING:

PRACTICAL PROJECTS FOR THE BEGINNER

THE BASIC GUIDE TO SEWING:

PRACTICAL PROJECTS FOR THE BEGINNER

Viking Sewing Machines Inc. / Sewing Information Resources
Westlake, Ohio   St. Charles, IL

A HUSQVARNA VIKING / SIR KEEPING THE WORLD SEWING BOOK

Sewing Information Resources
President: JoAnn Pugh-Gannon

Viking Sewing Machines Inc.
Senior Vice President Sales and Marketing: Stan Ingraham
Publicity Director: Nancy Jewell

THE BASIC GUIDE TO SEWING: PRACTICAL PROJECTS FOR BEGINNERS
was produced in conjunction with:
Production: Ernie Shelton, Shelton Design Studios
Photography: Kaz Ayukawa, K Graphics, Michael Hutchins, H/P Hutchins Photography
Sample making: Karen Kunkel, Gretchen McGinnis, Jean Knudsen, Nancy Keller
Index: Mary Helen Schiltz

Printed in China

ISBN 1-886884-10-2

TABLE OF CONTENTS

WHY DO YOU WANT TO SEW?

No doubt there are many underlying reasons you purchased this book—you want to decorate a new home or apartment, you want to add some fun pillows to your child's room, or you want to spruce up a window treatment in today's colors. But whatever the inspiration, the real reason you bought this book is to learn how to sew—quickly and easily. You probably own a sewing machine, a gift for graduation or a wedding, one that has been sitting in the closet for some time. Well, now is the time to learn how to use it.

With the plethora of discount and outlet stores in every community, sewing for economic reasons has almost become a thing of the past. No longer is it cheaper to make most garments for you or your family. Trends change quickly and with the demands on your time, making the time to sit down to sew gets lost in many people's agendas of running here and there.

However, not to discourage you before you even get started, let it be said that women and men sew today for many different reasons. Be it economics when it comes to decorating your home or the pure pleasure of being able to proudly say

"I made it myself", adults and children alike are still enjoying the art of sewing.

Decorating your home can become an expensive proposition. By being able to add the extra touches, such as special pillows, table covers or cover-ups, you can still save quite a bit of money and have fun doing it, too! As a beginner you may be intimidated with making elaborate window treatments, so start small with elegantly designed pillows from beautiful fabrics and trims. There are lots of ideas included here to get you started from pillows to pocketed shower curtains. The decision is yours.

The other reason people sew today is for the simple enjoyment of the art. They are expressing themselves through fabric and threads. Some are even making a living creating beautiful, one-of-a-kind quilts or wall hangings, while others design and sew wonderfully embellished garments. The pure enjoyment of working with fine fabrics, lovely threads, trims, or designs is the inspiration to create. Their sewing machine is their tool, just as a saw or hammer is to a carpenter. They have learned to use their tools (sewing machine, presser feet, and accessories) in the best possible ways.

Start here and follow the simple instructions given with each project, learning new techniques as you go along. This book is designed to help you learn as you sew. The specific techniques you will learn are highlighted and a brief list of terms is defined with each project helping you better understand what tasks, notions or tools you will be performing or using. A complete glossary is included in the back of the book for your easy reference. Make this book your sewer's bible referring back to it as you venture off into bigger, more involved projects.

You may be looking for a hobby or you have an idea for making a living. But either way, sewing can become an addiction. Often, our lives get out of control and we need to find something that centers us and we can call our own. Sewing can fill that spot. It is fun and relaxing and can be very creative. That's why we designed this book just for you, the beginner. We want you to experience the joy of feeling great fabrics, of blending colors and creating something wonderful for you or a friend, of beautifully decorating a room, or of hearing the joy of a child exclaiming over a colorful and playful nap mat. Have fun—enjoy sewing!

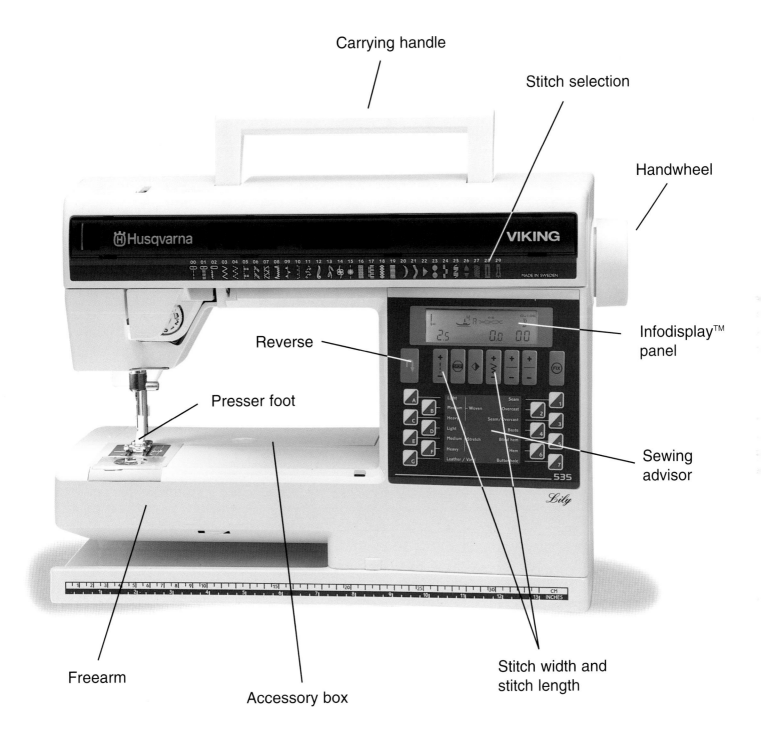

Carrying handle

Stitch selection

Handwheel

Reverse

Presser foot

Infodisplay™ panel

Sewing advisor

Freearm

Accessory box

Stitch width and stitch length

UNDERSTANDING YOUR SEWING MACHINE

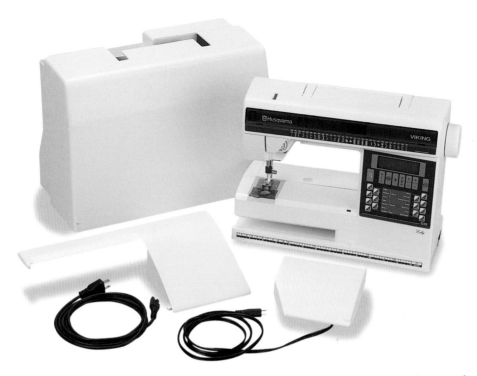

Your sewing machine is the most important tool involved in the completion of sewing projects. Knowledge of the parts and functions of your sewing machine will help boost your confidence. The key parts of most sewing machines are labeled on the basic model shown here. Refer to your sewing machine user's guide if the parts on your model look different. As you spend more time sewing, it will be natural to focus less on the operations of the machine and more on being creative!

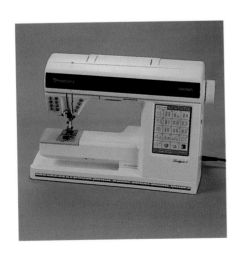

One of the best ways to learn about your sewing machine is to take hands-on classes. Most sewing machine retailers offer new owner's classes with the purchase of a new machine. For others who would like to learn more about the sewing machines they already own, basic sewing classes are ideal for gaining the fundamentals. These classes teach you everything from threading your sewing machine to using all the stitch capabilities on it.

Before you sew, be sure you are prepared to perform routine machine maintenance. Be able to thread the upper thread and wind and thread the bobbin. When your sewing machine is threaded correctly, you can expect good results. Two other tasks you will incur in the normal course of sewing are inserting new needles and changing presser feet.

With the presser foot lift in the up position and the needle at its highest point, begin threading your sewing machine. Slide a spool of thread on the spool pin. Draw the thread away from the spool under or over any thread guides. Bring the thread between the tension discs and up into the slot on the take-up lever. Draw the thread into the thread guide above the needle. Cut the end of the thread at an angle and thread the eye of the needle from front to back. Pull the thread approximately 5" away from the needle underneath to the side of the presser foot.

The Bobbin Case and Bobbins

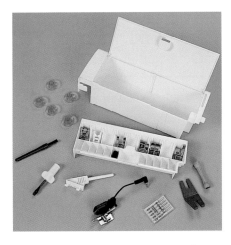

A stitch is formed when the needle carrying the upper thread pierces through the fabric into the bobbin area and locks with the lower thread. The bobbin is what holds the lower thread. Bobbins are made of plastic or metal, and can vary in size and appearance. Because sewing machine manufacturers design bobbins to fit into the bobbin cases of their specific models, remember to use only the bobbins that came with your sewing

machine. Using an incorrect bobbin will effect the look and quality of your stitch.

To prepare your bobbin for sewing, you will first need to wind a bobbin. Many sewing machines allow you to wind a bobbin directly from the needle onto the bobbin. Place a bobbin on the bobbin-winding spindle. Follow the illustration in your

HANDY HINT

When winding a bobbin, it is always best to wind thread onto an empty bobbin to maintain an even tension on the thread rather than wind over a partially filled bobbin.

user's guide for the threading path for your machine. Fill the bobbin by pressing on the foot control. Once the bobbin is full, slide the bobbin spindle over, if necessary, remove the bobbin, and cut the thread with the cutter. Always refer to your sewing machine user's guide for specific instructions on winding and threading a bobbin, as this procedure often varies from brand to brand.

There are two different types of bobbin cases, built-in and removable. Both types of cases have a tension spring that controls the tension on the

bobbin thread. The way you thread your bobbin will depend upon the type of bobbin case you have. Again, it is best to refer to your user's guide for instructions on threading your bobbin case. An incorrectly placed bobbin can affect your stitch quality.

Needles

It may be one of the smallest parts of the sewing machine, but the needle has a big influence on stitch quality. Several features make needles more than just a skinny piece of steel. A closer look reveals a thick part, the shank, and a smooth round middle, the shaft, which tapers to a point. Notice the shank has two distinct sides, one flat and the other round. On most sewing machines, the correct way to insert a needle is with the flat side of the needle shank facing away. The other features of the needle are the front groove, the eye, and the scarf.

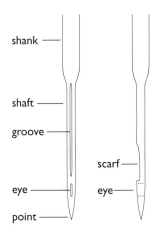

When you begin to shop for needles, you will notice there is an extensive selection. This is due to the wide variety of fabric we sew with today. The names and numbering system can be overwhelming. A sizing system is based on the diameter of the body, or shaft, of the needle. The European and American sizing system for needles have been combined so needle packaging bears two numbers, such as #80/12. An easy way to understand the needle sizing is the larger the number, the larger the needle. The general rule for choosing a needle for a project is to match the needle to the fabric–heavier fabrics demand larger needles. Conversely, lightweight fabrics should be sewn with a fine needle.

Although there are many specialty needles appropriate for unique fabrics, knowledge of three classifications of needles will cover most of your sewing needs. First, *Universal* needles are designed to sew on all woven fabrics. The *Universal* needle has a slightly rounded point and also will perform well on knits. The *Jeans* needle is ideal when sewing on heavy or densely woven fabrics. The third class, *Ballpoint* needles, have rounded points perfect for sewing knits.

Within each class of needles are numerous sizes to cover the weight of fabrics you may encounter. In many cases, there is more than one right needle to use. Experiment on your project fabric with possible needle choices and use the needle that makes the fewest obvious holes and produces the best stitch quality.

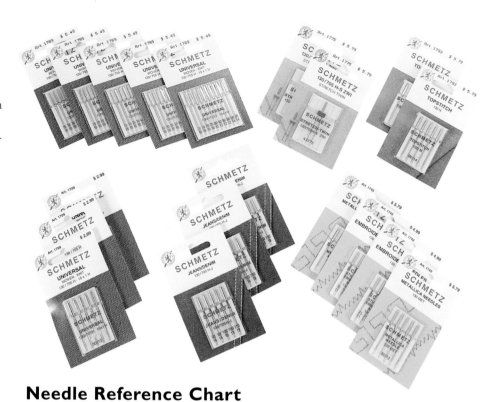

Needle Reference Chart

FABRIC	COMPATIBLE NEEDLE
Lightweight woven fabric Sheer, cotton, linen	Universal #70/10
Medium-weight woven fabric Muslin, quilting cotton, home decorating fabric, broadcloth, wool, linen, denim, corduroy	Universal #80/12 Jeans #80/12
Heavy-weight woven fabric Drapery, tapestry, duck, wool	Universal #90/14 Jeans #90/14
Lightweight knit Jersey, single knit, tricot	Stretch or Ballpoint #70/10 Universal #70/10
Medium-weight knit Sweatshirt fleece, lycra, spandex	Stretch or Ballpoint #80/12 Universal #80/12
Heavy-weight knit Sweatshirt fleece, polar knit, lycra	Stretch or Ballpoint #90/14 Universal #90/14

Good habits count when it comes to needles. First and foremost, use a needle compatible to the type and weight of your fabric. The GOLDEN RULE OF SEWING should be: *Begin each new project with a fresh needle.* Needles can develop burrs when you sew too fast, tug on the fabric, or hit a pin. Sew at a sensible speed. Develop a sensitive ear for your sewing; if you hear a pinging or popping noise, then its time to replace the problem needle. Sewing over pins is the biggest offense to your needle; the result can be nicks on the needle causing runs from the stitching line, a bent tip, or worse yet, a broken needle. As you approach pins, stop sewing to remove them.

HANDY HINT

Make it easy on yourself – always insert pins into the fabric perpendicular to the edge with the heads sticking out. You can quickly remove the pins while you are sewing.

Even if you are good to your needle, you need to keep in mind that needles will become dull after hours of sewing. Remember the GOLDEN RULE OF SEWING.

Presser Feet

The purpose of the presser foot is to hold the fabric against the feed teeth while you are sewing. It can be lifted and lowered with the presser foot lift. Always lower the presser foot before you begin sewing to engage the upper thread tension.

Choosing the right presser foot to sew with is almost as important as choosing the right shoes to wear with an outfit. The presser feet that come with your machine are designed to make the many different sewing tasks easier and more precise. Newer sewing machines come with an array of presser feet. The Husqvarna Viking Lily, model 535, sewing machine has an Infodisplay™ window on the front of the machine that suggests the best foot to use based on your stitch selection and fabric type and weight. If your sewing machine does not have a display, it helps to learn the intended use for the standard presser feet. Several feet can be considered multitasking feet.

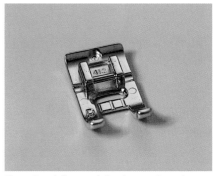

Standard foot with channel and center mark: for overlock and decorative stitches, satin stitches

Buttonhole foot: for sewing buttonholes, adding elastic cording under bridging stitch, and sewing invisible zippers

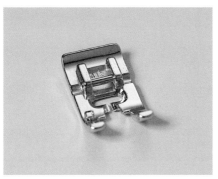

Standard foot: for straight and stretch stitch, zigzag

Blindhem foot: for sewing blindhems, topstitching, and edgestitching

Zipper foot: for sewing zippers and piping

Overcast foot: for overcasting and seaming

Buttonhole sensor foot: buttonhole foot capable of sewing consecutive same-sized buttonholes using sensor

Machine Care and Troubleshooting

It only takes a few finished projects to realize the sewing machine is your best friend. To ensure your sewing machine continues to run smooth, regularly brush away visible and hidden lint. Slide off the stitch plate and use a small brush included with most sewing machines to remove lint around the feed teeth and bobbin case. Do not use canned air, or similar products, to resolve the lint problem. Canned air complicates the lint buildup by blowing it deeper inside your sewing machine. Husqvarna Viking is a brand of sewing machines that requires no oiling since the metal parts have permanent embedded lubrication. If you own another brand, check your sewing machine user's guide for instruction on oiling.

Another important aspect of machine care is regular servicing by an authorized sewing machine retailer. It is a good practice to have your sewing machine serviced at least once or twice a year depending on how much you sew.

Most sewing machine user's guides have a troubleshooting section located in the back of the manual. If you are experiencing any problems with your stitch quality, check that section before calling your authorized repair person. You can often solve the problem yourself by following a short checklist. Check your threading, check your bobbin and bobbin case, check your presser foot lift, and check your needle.

Experiment with your standard presser feet and you may find a new use for a foot. But many other optional specialty presser feet are available for creative sewing endeavors like appliqué, quilting, and heirloom sewing. Stop by your local sewing machine retailer to learn more about these feet.

To change the presser foot, first make sure the presser foot lift is up and the needle is in the highest position. Some brands of sewing machines may have presser feet that snap on and off, a presser foot release button, or a screw to loosen and tighten. Check the user's guide to see how the feet are changed on your sewing machine.

USING YOUR SEWING MACHINE STITCHES

Using all the stitches means you will be getting the most from your sewing machine. You must first understand how to choose stitches. On many new sewing machine models, stitches are selected by touching a button and then the stitch length and width are automatically set. If your sewing machine has levers or dials, check the user's guide for instructions on stitch selection. Learn about the stitches on your sewing machine and what they were designed to do. Once you understand the practical uses for stitches, challenge yourself to use the stitches creatively. The more you use the stitches, the more you will really feel like you are sewing.

What Is Each Stitch?

The stitches built into the basic sewing machine shown on page 8 are listed below. These stitches seem to be the standard package on most brands for a mid-line machine, give or take a few stitches. If you own a different machine, compare your stitches to those listed here.

Reinforced Straight Stitch: for seams subject to considerable strain, for instance, to reinforce and topstitch sportswear and work clothes, 25 different needle positions possible

Zigzag: for fine rolled edge, lace edging, finishing seams, and satin stitching

Straight Stitch: for sewing on all weights of woven fabrics, 25 different needle positions possible

Stretch Stitch: for seams on tricot knit and stretch fabrics

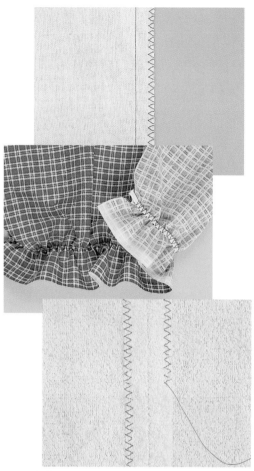

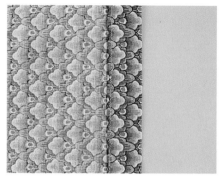

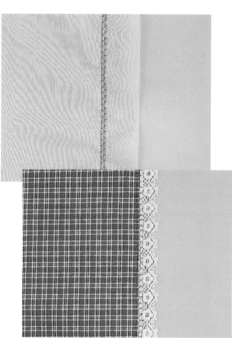

Blindhem Stitch: for invisible hems in woven and stretch medium- to heavy-weight fabrics

Overlock Stitch: seam and overcast in one step, for medium and heavy stretch fabrics

3-Step Zigzag: for overcasting the edge, mending, sewing on patches, sewing on terry cloth, and sewing on elastic

Flatlock Stitch: for decorative hems and overlapped seams, belts, and bands

Bridging Stitch: for joining two pieces of fabric with finished edges and for elastic shirring

Overcast Stitch: seam and overcast in one step, for light stretch and non-stretch fabrics

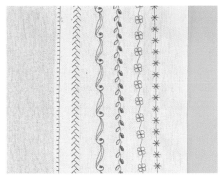

Decorative Stitches: for decorating clothing, crafts, gifts, and home décor

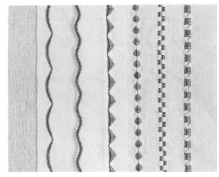

Decorative Edging or Satin Stitches: for adding shaped satin decorative edging after trimming, compact decorative satin stitches for decorating clothing, crafts, gifts, and home décor

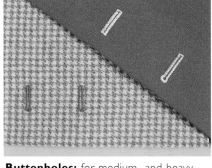

Buttonholes: for medium- and heavy-weight fabrics in keyhole or square-ended

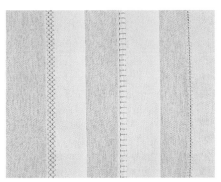

Hemstitches: for hemstitching often used with a wing needle on natural fiber fabrics

Tapered Satin Stitch: for appliqué or decorative trimming with automatic tapering to start and finish stitching, for monogramming

Depending on the model of machine you own and its sophistication, you will possess more or fewer stitches. The most modern, up-to-date sewing machines available today have unlimited possibilities and can be updated with new stitches and functions via a computer disk or over the Internet. As you sew more, your desires for more machine functions and capabilities will grow.

Pre-programmed Satin Stitch: for appliqué, sewing on laces and bands

Pre-programmed Darning Stitch: Darn and mend work clothes, tablecloths, and linen towels

What Is Perfect Tension?

The simple translation of perfect tension is when the needle and bobbin threads lock exactly in the middle of the layers of fabric you are sewing. Tension affects the stitch quality. If the tension on one thread is greater than the other thread, then the tension is uneven. The thread with the looser tension floats on one side and the seam can be either very weak or puckered. Ideally, the tension on both threads is equal so you have the strongest seam possible.

Many sewing machines provide suggested tension settings on a display on the front of the machine for each fabric and stitch selection you make. And top-of-the-line sewing machines offer automatic tension settings–you choose your fabric and stitch and the tension is set for you.

To check the tension on your sewing machine, thread your machine with one color of thread.on top through the needle and another color on the bobbin. Take two pieces of a medium-weight woven fabric and sew a seam. You will have perfect tension when you see only one color of thread on each side of your fabrics. Your sewing machine may have a tension dial located on the top or

front or a digital display for changing the tension. Make small incremental changes on the dial, stitch on two layers of fabric after each change, and check the results. If after making minor changes to the tension dial you cannot arrive at a balanced tension, take your sewing machine to your authorized repair person for an adjustment.

As you work with different types of fabrics and stitches, it is necessary to test the tension. When you are sewing a satin stitch or decorative stitches with rayon or metallic thread in the needle and a lightweight bobbin thread (60 wt. bobbin thread), the difference in thread weight will cause an imperfect tension. The decorative thread should be pulled slightly to the wrong side of the fabric and the bobbin thread should not be visible from the right side of the fabric.

Stitch Length and Width

The stitch length and width are two aspects of any stitch. You may need to alter the stitch length or width based on different types or weights of fabric. For example, a straight stitch on a lightweight, woven fabric should be sewn at a length of 2.0 mm (12-15 stitches per inch) while the same stitch on a heavy-weight, woven fabric should be sewn at a longer length of 3.0 mm (8-10 stitches per inch). In general, as the fabric weight increases, so should the stitch length and width, if necessary.

The width setting on your sewing machine can help you move your straight and stretch stitches for perfect positioning. Get comfortable with changing the width of your stitch. As with the length, the width of your

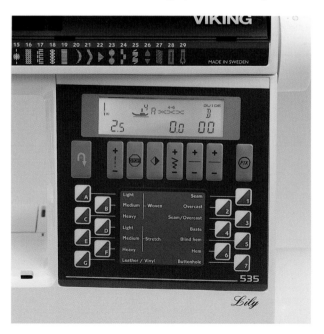

stitch is affected by the weight of the fabric. As the stitch becomes wider, the more chances the fabric will pucker. Either reduce your stitch width or stabilize the fabric underneath with a stabilizing fabric.

When a stitch is selected on new sewing machines, displays like the one shown give the automatic setting for the stitch length and width. If your sewing machine does not have this feature, test new stitches on scrap fabric before using the stitches on your project. Check the user's guide for additional information on stitch length and width settings for your sewing machine.

The stitch length and width is not only a means for making stitches appropriate for various weights of fabrics, but it also is a way to bring a new look to decorative stitches. Experiment with the settings for fun results.

Needle Positions

On most sewing machines, you have the capability of moving your needle to the right or left of center. This feature is particularly handy when you are edgestitching or topstitching close to the edge of the fabric. Some machines have a specific button for this feature while others have you adjust your width setting. Check your user's guide for the specific details on how to move your needle.

For most of the projects in this book, a ½" seam allowance is used. The stitch plates of European sewing machines have metric markings, so the lines provide for these seam allowances: 10 mm = ⅜" and 15 mm = ⅝". Move your needle position all the way to the right, or 6.0 mm, and then adjust it to 4.0mm. Sew with the edge of the fabric along the 15 mm line for a ½" seam allowance.

Starting and Stopping

Nothing can be more frustrating than a seam started with a thread jam or the thread pulling out of the needle when you start to sew. Taking your first stitch on fabric will eliminate thread jams. To prevent the thread from pulling out of the eye of the needle leave a substantial thread tail for both needle and bobbin thread (about 4"-5") laying under the presser foot toward the back of the machine. If you have a thread cutter, draw the threads up and over the cutter to hold them while starting.

When you are sewing a seam, first place the edge of the fabric underneath the needle and lower the presser foot. Sew forward two or three stitches and then reverse two or three stitches. The reverse is a stitch function on the sewing machine operated by pushing a button or turning a dial. Backstitching prevents your seam from unraveling. Continue the seam by sewing to the opposite edge of the fabric. End the seam by backstitching as you did to begin the seam. Lift the presser foot and pull the fabric, needle, and bobbin threads 5" away from the foot. Cut the threads away from the edge of the fabric. Clip your threads at the start and finish of each seam to keep the project looking neat.

A different technique is used to start and stop decorative stitching. Rather than using the reverse feature to secure the ends of the thread, most new sewing machines have a FIX or locking stitch, which ties the needle and bobbin thread on the back side of fabric. Touch this button to begin and end your decorative stitching. If your sewing machine is not equipped with this function, simply reduce your stitch length to 0 when starting and stopping decorative stitching. Stitch a few stitches in place and then adjust the stitch length to the normal setting. Some stitches, such as buttonholes, have a built-in locking stitch as part of the procedure.

SETTING UP YOUR
SEWING AREA

*Remember, as a beginner, it is not necessary to invest in a lot of
cabinetry and storage until you are sure you will continue sewing. The
dining room or kitchen table or a desk in a bedroom will work well as a
sewing surface. We have all probably started out by cutting out our patterns
on the floor. A good storage box for your supplies can be tucked in the
closet or under the bed when you are finished. Choose a comfortable chair
to avoid aching shoulders and make sure your sewing area is well lit.*

Whether you have the luxury of devoting an entire room to your sewing addiction or have to pull your machine out of the closet each time you want to begin a new project, there are some simple things to remember to make your sewing a pleasurable experience. Your seating comfort, proper lighting, and supply storage become important aspects in a sewer's life. Since we can all dream...let's explore a few ways for setting up an efficient sewing area.

A small corner of the basement, attic, or your family room can be the ideal sewing area. Place a cutting table between a pillar and wall to divide your space from the rest of the room. This surface, if covered with a countertop laminate, can double as a serving area for parties after the cutting mat is removed. The cutting table should be at a comfortable height to your size for best use.

There are many types of sewing machine cabinets and tables available today. For the more sophisticated sewer, an additional space is needed for the overlock machine. The cabinet pieces shown here fit nicely into the corner utilizing the space well. Handy storage areas are incorporated into the doors.

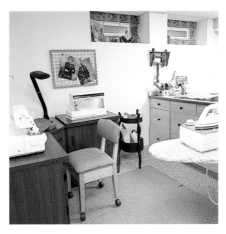

With the doors closed and the extensions folded in, the cabinet pieces can be rolled out of the way if necessary. The machines can fold down into the cabinet keeping busy fingers out of your equipment when you aren't using it. Another cabinet answer is inexpensive new or used office furniture. Small computer tables found at your local discount retailer are often the perfect solution as a sewing table. Pick out what is best for your space and remember to include wheels if straightening up each time you sew is a necessity.

A comfortable chair is also very important when sewing. Many sewer's select rolling desk chairs with adjustable seats, backs, and arms for true comfort. Your arms should be able to rest on the sewing machine table without straining your shoulders.

Good lighting in your sewing area is of the utmost importance. Of course, natural light is wonderful but project lighting is also important. An adjustable lamp that clamps to the work surface or stands on the floor can spotlight right on the sewing area around the presser foot on your machine. If you have to deal with fluorescent light, try to find tubes that simulate natural light to reduce eyestrain.

Your cutting table can perform double duty if you incorporate drawers or shelves underneath. If a permanent cutting table is an option for you, consider using kitchen cabinetry found at your do-it-yourself lumber yards. Set up the drawers to your specifications. Deeper drawers are great for lining up patterns.

Storage is a vital part of sewing. The more you sew the more you will find that you are buying fabric just because you like it rather than with a specific project in mind. If you are a true fabri-holic, storage of your great "finds" becomes a necessity. Wall shelves with baskets or boxes are great for the stacks of wonderful fabrics you have collected. Be sure to take extra care with woolens to avoid moth holes. If shelves are not an option, again the local container or discount retail store will have great rolling shelves of all sizes that can easily be tucked away in a closet.

Shallow drawers with drawer dividers are perfect for storing the many threads you will accumulate over time. Again the local container or discount retail store is the perfect place to find these handy dividers.

There are many types of irons on the market today from steam generators to the every-day steam variety. Most sewers prefer one with good steam capacity and a stainless steel sole for easy gliding. Auto-shut-off becomes a matter of preference and convenience.

The more you sew, the more equipment you may acquire. With the introduction of embroidery machines to the home sewing market, more space is needed to accommodate the computer and scanner along with the sewing machine and embroidery set-up. As you begin to sew more and more, you will find that you will need more space for your passion!

And last but not least, you will need an area for pressing. We recommend that you press as you sew a seam or area. This method of sewing makes your final project look more professional. An adjustable sturdy ironing board can be purchased in many places. Make sure you have leveled the legs if you are setting it up on carpet.

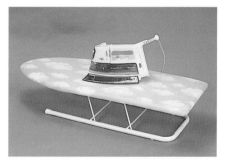

But if space is an issue, a tabletop ironing board works very well. Place this small board on the dining room or kitchen table and let the extended surface support the excess fabric while you are pressing.

IMPORTANT NOTIONS AND TOOLS

When you begin to sew, you will need to purchase a few supplies to get you started. As with anything, the more you get into a project the more supplies you can buy – all to make the job easier! We will let you make that determination for yourself however; there are a few important notions that you will need immediately.

Thread

We have already discussed the importance of the needle to your sewing in the section Understanding Your Sewing Machine. But without its companion, good-quality thread, you will not be able to do much sewing.

There are many different kinds of thread you can buy and many different reasons for so many kinds. For most practical purposes, you will need a good-quality polyester or cotton-wrapped polyester thread for the projects in this book. But let's explore the threads that are available in most sewing stores today.

First, we recommend that you dispose of any old spools of thread you may own at this time. By old, we mean, 100% cotton thread that has been passed down from your mother or grandmother for you to use "when you start to sew." You certainly can

keep the spools for their antique value (especially if they are wooden spools) but the sewing value of this thread is minimal as most likely it is dried out and fragile.

The following chart gives you an overall view of the most common threads you may discover in your shopping trips. In most sewing stores you will find either cotton-wrapped polyester or 100% polyester thread for all-purpose sewing. These threads are strong, ideal for most fabrics, and

suitable for any sewing machine. Select the proper thread for the fabric you are working on.

It is advisable to buy name brand threads rather than bargain-bin specials for their overall quality and durability. Your stitch quality is just as dependent on the thread as it is on the correct needle for what you are sewing. If you remember to use quality fabrics, threads, and notions, your finished project will also display that quality image.

THREAD TYPES	USES
100% polyester or cotton-wrapped polyester	All-purpose sewing on most weights of fabric
100% cotton – extra fine	Lightweight fabrics such as batiste, chiffon, organza, etc., fine silks
Rayon	Machine embroidery, appliqué, and decorative work
Topstitching/Buttonhole Twist – cotton-covered polyester, 100% polyester, or silk	Topstitching on wools, sewing on buttons, buttonholes
100% cotton quilting thread	Quilting
100% nylon Upholstery and Home Decorating thread	Used on very heavy upholstery fabrics, duck, and canvas

Pinning, Marking, and Cutting

Again the choices are unlimited in this category of notions. There are many types of pins and marking pens or pencils. Spend some time in the notions department of your local fabric store exploring the wide selection.

An item every home should have, whether you sew or not, is a magnetic pincushion. This handy tool keeps your pins organized and at your fingertips. Keep it right next to your machine as you sew.

Pattern tracing paper that is squared in a 1" grid is a valuable supply to buy for making patterns, as we do often in this book. The grided lines help you keep everything square and on grain. This notion is purchased by the yard.

HANDY HINT

For the handyman of the house, the magnetic pincushion keeps small screws or nails right on the job sight without getting lost. And if anything gets dropped on the floor, swipe the magnet over the area and your lost pins or screws are picked up in a minute!

There are many types of marking tools for you to choose from. Chalk pencils and markers, air- and water-soluble pens, and tracing wheels and tracing paper are some of the types you will find. Before and during construction, you will need to transfer marks from the pattern tissue, or possibly measure and mark the fabric. Test the marking tool on the selvedge of the fabric to make sure the mark can be seen during sewing and easily removed afterwards.

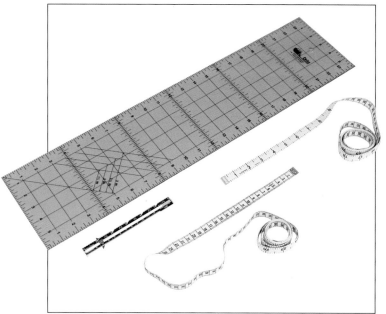

A clear plastic ruler, a seam gauge, and a tape measure are essential tools for your sewing box. You will use them frequently and you should have all three on hand. Purchase a coated tape measure that won't stretch or tear with use.

Good-quality scissors will make your cutting process much easier. Purchase 7" or 8" high-quality steel scissors and keep them only for cutting fabric. Cutting anything other than fabric with your fabric scissors will quickly dull them. There are a variety of other styles of scissors, such as pinking shears, embroidery scissors, thread clips, or buttonhole scissors, designed to do specific jobs. As you sew more, you may want to acquire other styles.

Another cutting tool is the rotary cutter and mat. Most often used by quilters, this tool is similar to a pizza cutter and is used with a special mat and ruler.

HANDY HINT

There are both left- and right-handed scissors available for more comfortable cutting.

Additional Tools

There are a few other tools that may help make your sewing easier. We have used some of them on the projects described here.

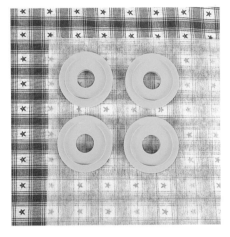

Dressmaker weights can be used instead of pins when cutting out your pattern pieces. If you are concerned about pin holes in your fabric, use weights instead.

A tube turner, shown here, is another great tool you may not want to be without. With all the tabs used in the projects in this book, the largest-sized tube turner would come in handy.

HANDY HINT

A seam gauge and a seam ripper are often included with the accessories that come with your sewing machine. Check first before you buy.

A seam ripper and a buttonhole cutter become essential notions the more you sew. Not that you will have to remove seams very often but a seam ripper can also be used to carefully open buttonholes.

HOW TO CHOOSE A PATTERN

A variety of projects have been included in this book to get you started sewing for yourself, your family, and your home. For more ideas and inspiration, the pattern catalog is a wonderful source. Patterns offer step-by-step guidance to complete a project. The techniques illustrated in this book will apply to many of the more complicated projects you decide to take on.

The Catalog and The Catalog Page

Take some time when visiting your local fabric store to page through the current pattern books. New patterns are developed ten times a year, so you are likely to find the same clothing styles, crafts, and home decorating items you currently see in the department stores. Pattern catalogs are a great source for the latest trends in fabric and accessories.

Selecting a pattern can seem daunting for the beginner. It is best to remember to keep it simple. Begin by choosing a style or project that you really like. Look for design details that are at your sewing skill level. Special pattern logos help alert you to skill level or degree of difficulty, and the time it would take to make the project. The beginner sewer will find

many patterns on "quick and easy" sewing in the current pattern catalogs.

As you scan the numerous pages of the catalog, you will notice that patterns are grouped together in a variety of ways. There are categories for clothing (dresses, coordinates, sleep wear, or bridal), home decorating, crafts, as well as special-size ranges for garment sewing, for example, large sizes, children, men, and boys. All of the major pattern companies have their own terms or logos to indicate specialized patterns. For descriptions of each pattern category, turn to the back of the catalog.

The catalog page offers information to get you started. The photo, whether fashion or home decorating and crafts, will show how the pattern looks after it is sewn. Consider the

photo an accurate guide as to how the pattern looks when completed. The photo also provides information as to fabric selection, textures, and fabric pattern mixes that are suitable for the particular pattern.

Often the catalog page includes an illustration of other views or options. These drawings help point out specifics as to stitching and fitting details as well as offer further inspiration and fabric ideas. Also included on the page is a pattern number and a brief description of the pattern. The catalog page will list the size the pattern comes in (for clothing) and generally, how much fabric is needed (the specific yardage is listed on the back of the pattern envelope). Back views may be included to show details of the item that are not visible from a photo or illustration.

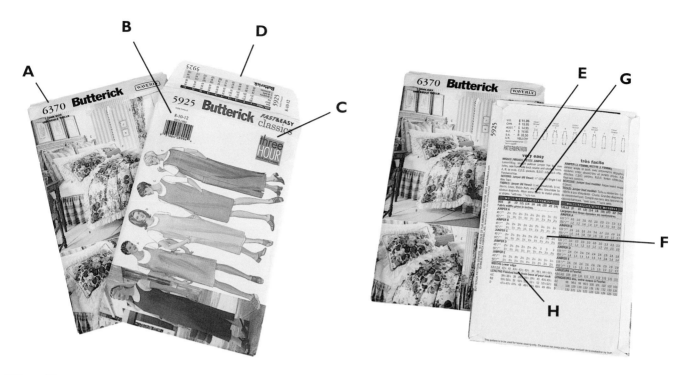

The Pattern Envelope

The pattern envelope *front* contains some of the same information as the catalog page but in greater detail. The envelope front will have the same photograph and/or sketch that is featured on the catalog page as well as the pattern number (A), the size (B), and any logos (C). Sometimes the number of pattern pieces will be listed. The flap (D) on garment patterns includes a pattern-sizing chart with bust, waist, and hip measurements per size.

For garment and many craft patterns, the envelope *back* is your shopping list. Home decorating patterns, however, include this information in detail within the envelope. Whether on the back or on the inside of the pattern envelope, information including yardage amounts, notions, and supplies needed to make the pattern is given. Some of the information on the catalog page is

repeated such as the pattern number, number of pattern pieces, and back views. More complete information is given in the pattern description such as the different views and construction details not obvious on the pattern photograph or illustration.

A suggested fabric list (E) is given as a guide for shopping. It is a good idea to keep within these fabric suggestions as most have be tested by the pattern companies and promise to give the best results for that design.

The yardage chart (F), both in inches and centimeters, tells you how much fabric to purchase for the particular view desired by size and fabric width. For garment patterns, standard body measurements are included on the envelope as a reference for sizing patterns to fit your body. For home decorating patterns, such as window treatments, you will need to do some calculating prior to purchasing your fabric since the curtain or drape will

be custom made for your window. A diagram asking for specific measurements required is included on the instructions guide sheet. A measurement chart will help you record the measurements for your window and information on how to calculate yardage amounts.

A list of notions (G) is given. These will be all the additional items such as buttons, cording, loop and hook fasteners, or batting that are needed to complete the project. It is a good idea to purchase all the notions needed before you begin the project.

Finished garment measurements (H) are given on the envelope back. They are also useful in determining how the garment will look when stitched and whether you will need to make adjustments before cutting. Metric equivalents of this information are also listed on a separate chart opposite the Imperial measurements.

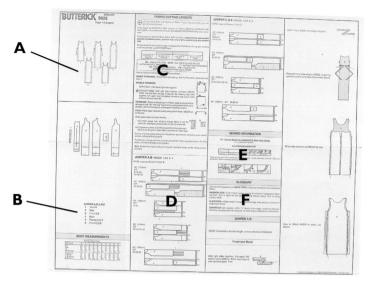

A

B

C

D

E

F

Inside The Envelope

The pattern envelope contains the instruction guide sheet(s) and tissue pattern pieces necessary to make the garment, craft, or home decorating project.

The instruction sheet gives detailed information to guide your sewing step-by-step from cutting to construction. It is a good idea to pull out the guide before purchasing a pattern to give you an idea of all that is involved. Check to see if there are many new techniques you haven't learned and if it is within your skill level. The instructions will also give you an estimate of how long it will take to complete the pattern.

Before beginning any project, read through the guide sheet carefully. Review the steps and be sure you understand each one. For new techniques, refer to the pages in this book for help. This will save time and frustration later on.

The guide sheet will give you complete information beginning with:
Line Drawings (A): These drawings are simple sketches of the views included in the pattern. They give you

the technical details of the particular design.

Pattern Pieces (B): These too are simplified sketches of each pattern piece. Each piece will be numbered or lettered, and below the drawings is a list of each number or letter and what each piece is (for example, #1 - Bodice Front). Each view will be listed separately.

Fabric Cutting Layouts (C): This section begins with a key that explains common pattern symbols and how to make simple adjustments if necessary. Tips are given for cutting and marking techniques such as working WITH NAP.

HANDY HINT

Knit fabrics have surface texture and will always use a WITH NAP layout.

Cutting Layout Views (D): These layouts will show you how to position

the actual pattern pieces on your fabric. The drawings are computer-generated and are designed to give you the layout that requires the least amount of fabric. Cutting layouts are given for a variety of fabric widths and for each view. It is important to identify your correct view before cutting. Draw a circle around your view so you can easily refer to it. Be sure to pay attention to WITH NAP layouts. This refers to fabric with a one-way design, pile, or surface texture. These layouts will have the pattern pieces all running in the same direction.

HANDY HINT

Many patterns today are multisized and the pattern tissues have multiple cutting lines. Select the correct cutting line for your size and highlight it with a marker to make your cutting accurate.

Sewing Information (E): This section defines some common sewing techniques such as size of seam allowances, trimming and clipping techniques, pressing know-how, and more. Also included is an illustration shading key describing the right side and wrong side of the fabric, lining, interfacing, and underlining.

Glossary (F): A short glossary or dictionary of terms follows the Sewing Information. Two to three terms that you will encounter while sewing this project are defined.

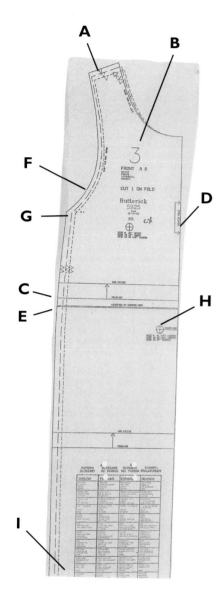

The Pattern Pieces

The individual pattern pieces include valuable information to the home sewer. Each contains directions and symbols that aid you in the sewing process. These symbols include:

Notches (A): These are triangular markings on the cutting line drawn into the seam allowance. When cutting out your pattern, cut the triangles out from the cutting line.

These markings are used for matching two pieces in construction.

Letters or Numbers (B): Letters or numbers are boldly printed on each pattern piece to identify one piece from another by view. They are usually numbered in the order in which they are used.

Solid Lines (C): Solid lines will show you where to place pockets and buttonholes, and also designate the outer cutting line and fold lines.

Grainline Arrow: This solid line with arrowheads at each end is used to place the pattern pieces on the straight grain of fabric. Measure an even distance from the selvedge raw edge, or fold to the arrow to position the pattern piece parallel to the edge of the fabric.

Bent Grainline Arrow (D): The squared-off or bent arrow indicates that the pattern piece must be placed on a fabric fold. The fabric is not cut along this line.

Lengthen or Shorten Lines (E): These two parallel lines allow you to lengthen or shorten a pattern piece without distorting its shape.

Cutting Lines (F): These are the solid and broken lines along the outer edge of the pattern piece used for cutting. As many patterns are now printed with more than one size, refer to your correct pattern size before cutting to ensure you are using the correct lines for your size.

Seamlines: These broken lines usually placed ⅝" from the cutting lines indicate the seamlines. Multisized patterns and most home decorating pattern pieces will not include marked seamlines on the tissue.

Dots or Circles (G): Small dots or circles are used for matching pattern pieces during construction. They may also indicate placement of design details such as darts.

Large Circle with Cross (H): This symbol indicates the bust point and the waistline or hipline.

Darts: Shown as V-shaped broken lines with a circle or dots at the end. Darts add shape to a flat piece of fabric.

Hem (I): Hem allowances are written out on the pattern pieces to tell you how much fabric to turn up.

TYPES OF FABRIC

The choices of fabric to sew with today are unlimited. You are able to almost duplicate what you see in ready-to-wear garments or in home decorating magazines immediately. Your trip to the fabric store may seem overwhelming at first, but if you take your time and look at all the selections, the task of choosing the right fabric won't seem so daunting. Tour the entire store identifying the areas for home decorating, fashion sewing, and quilting fabrics. Find the threads, patterns, and notions. There is a lot to look at and absorb.

Once you have decided on the project or pattern you want to sew, refer to the fabric suggestions given here or the ones provided by the pattern company. As a beginner, it is best to select the same type of fabric as listed to avoid any unnecessary difficulties. If you have any questions identifying the fabrics, ask someone in the store for assistance.

The fabrics you will be working with can be divided into two categories, fashion/quilting or home decorating. Fashion fabrics range in width from approximately 36" to 60". Home decorating fabrics are generally heavier in weight and wider in width (up to 110"-120") than fashion fabrics. Upholstery fabrics will be much heavier and often have a special backing for durability. The fiber content for both could include cotton, wool, linen, rayon, or other synthetics.

HANDY HINT

The ease of cleaning your garment or project should be taken into consideration, so check the end of the bolt for the fiber content before you buy.

Most of the projects in this book can be made from either fashion or home decorating fabric. But, you may have to piece the fashion fabrics more often to achieve the width needed for the pattern pieces. You may notice that the fashion fabrics are grouped in the store by types, such as wool tweeds, wool flannels, suit weight linen, or quilting calicos. The quilting cottons will also be sorted by color for matching and coordinating prints.

Home decorating fabrics are often grouped by color or groups of coordinates are displayed together to make your selection easier in planning a whole room. Take advantage of these groupings or colorways when choosing your fabric, as the manufacturer has taken some of the guesswork out of the job for you. You will notice on the edge of a home decorating printed fabric a series of small colored dots and possibly the collection name. These

dots indicate the different colored screens used to print the fabric, and the dots and name serve as a guide for matching coordinating solids and prints. Have fun mixing and matching your fabrics.

Knit fabrics are also readily available for fashion sewing and in a range of fiber combinations. However, they require slightly different handling and techniques in sewing. As a beginner, we would suggest you select a woven fabric of a reasonable weight for your first projects to ensure success.

Important Fabric Terms

Once you have selected your fabric—a wool, a cotton calico, a silk or maybe a home decorating fabric—you will need to understand some fabric terms before laying out the pattern and cutting. Woven fabric consists of threads worked in two directions (lengthwise and crosswise) over and under each other.

HANDY HINT

Most fashion fabrics are folded in half, selvedge to selvedge, and rolled on the bolt. Home decorating fabrics are usually rolled on a long tube in a single layer.

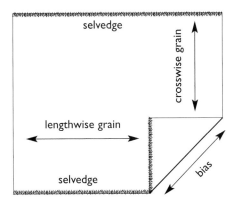

SELVEDGE (or SELVAGE): The tightly woven edges that run along the two lengthwise sides of the fabric.

GRAIN: Direction in which the threads are woven. **Lengthwise grain** runs parallel to the selvedge. **Crosswise grain** runs from selvedge to selvedge. There is usually a small amount of stretch to the crosswise grain. **Bias** is the diagonal across the lengthwise and crosswise threads. A true bias is at a 45-degree angle to any straight lengthwise or crosswise edge.

NAP: A finishing technique applied to fabric where the fibers lie flat in one direction. Understanding nap is important when sewing with corduroy, velvets, suede or suede-like fabrics, to name a few.

Stripes, Plaids, and Prints

As you read through the many projects in this book, you will discover we have not shied away from using bold prints, stripes, or plaids. As a beginner, if you understand how to match patterns from the start, using these wonderful fabrics will not be a problem for you.

There are different kinds of plaid that you should be aware of, *even* and *uneven*. To determine what kind of plaid you are working with, first fold the fabric back as you would for a true bias. **Even plaids** match up and are the same in both directions. **Uneven plaids** do not match in both directions. Some uneven plaids appear *even* at first but do not make a mirror image on repeat. A **repeat** is the distance between designs before they start again. The term, repeat, is most often used with home decorating fabrics. The instructions for matching prints are described in the project, *Reversible Patio Tablecloth*. Follow this same technique for matching plaids. Matching stripes is handled in E*asy Bistro Chair Cover*. Follow these instructions whenever you are dealing with prints, plaids, or stripes.

The Inside Story

Some projects you will encounter will call for a lining or interfacing. It is important to understand the difference between the two.

Linings are almost like a second skin, giving the garment or project a finished look and protecting it from wear. It prevents stretching and will add body to lighterweight fabrics. Linings add life to curtains and drapes, reduce wrinkling in garments, and hide the inner construction from view. You can use the same outer fabric for your lining or choose something slightly lighter in weight than the fashion or home decorating fabric. When a piece is reversible, the reverse side acts as the lining.

Interfacing provides shape and stability to the garment or home decorating project. It is usually used on areas such as collars, cuffs, facings, and waistbands. It adds stability to the header on drapes or curtains. Knit fabrics are interfaced to prevent stretching in certain areas, such as at a neckline.

There are two types of interfacings, sew-in and fusible, and both types can be woven, non-woven, or knit. Follow the manufacturer's instructions for applying each type. Select an interfacing appropriate to the weight of the fabric and where it will be used. Also remember to check the care label before you purchase the interfacing. It should be compatible to the care you will give your project. Test the interfacing on a scrap of your fabric before you work with it.

PILLOWS, CUSHIONS, & CHAIR COVERS

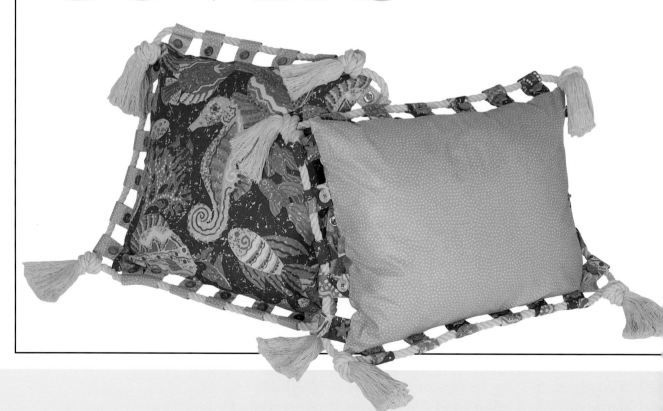

BASIC ACCENT
PILLOW

This simple knifed-edge pillow can be made any size or shape,

such as square, rectangle, and round or heart-shaped.

VOCABULARY

Press—to apply pressure to fabric making or setting creases or opening seam allowances using a temperature-controlled iron.

Seam Allowance—the remaining fabric left after a seam is sewn.

Slipstitch—simple hand stitch used to close an opening with small invisible stitches.

Trim—to cut away excess fabric from the seam allowance, corners, or curves for easier turning and pressing.

Turn—to reverse the sides of the fabric, such as "turn to the right side".

TECHNIQUES
YOU WILL LEARN

- Trimming
- Pressing
- Turning
- Slipstitch

Fabric: Decorator fabric—yardage based on pillow size

Notions: Matching sewing thread

    Fabric marking pen

    Ruler or tape measure

    Dressmaker pins

Needles: Universal needles #80/12

Other suppies: Pillow form of desired shape and size

1 Measure the length and width of your pillow form. Cut two squares or rectangles of fabric 1" larger than the desired finished pillow size (this allows ½" seam allowance on all sides).

HANDY
HINT

The standard seam allowance used for home decorating projects is ½" wide. The seam allowance typically used for garment construction is ⅝" wide.

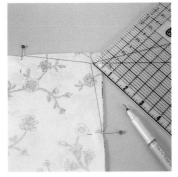

3 Using a fabric marker, mark ½" in diagonally from the corner. Draw lines connecting the pins to the corner marking.

2 To prevent the finished pillow from having floppy "dog-ear" corners, fold each fabric square in quarters. Measure and pin 4" from each side of the open corner through all thicknesses.

continued

4 Following the marked line, rim any excess fabric away through all thicknesses. Repeat this procedure on the back fabric.

5 With right sides together, stitch the pillow front and back together using a ½" seam leaving a 4" opening for turning and stuffing.

6 Trim the seam allowance across the corners to eliminate any bulk. Turn the fabric right side out and press the edges.

7 Insert the pillow form through the opening and slipstitch closed.

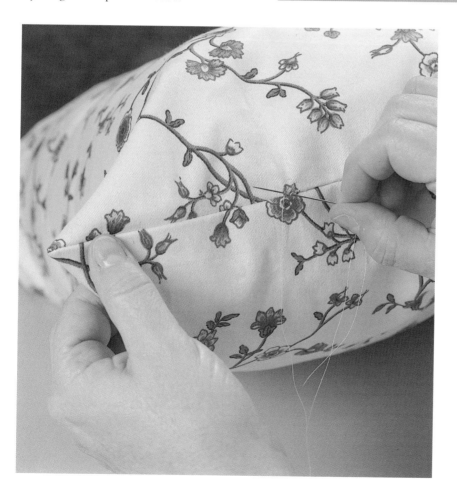

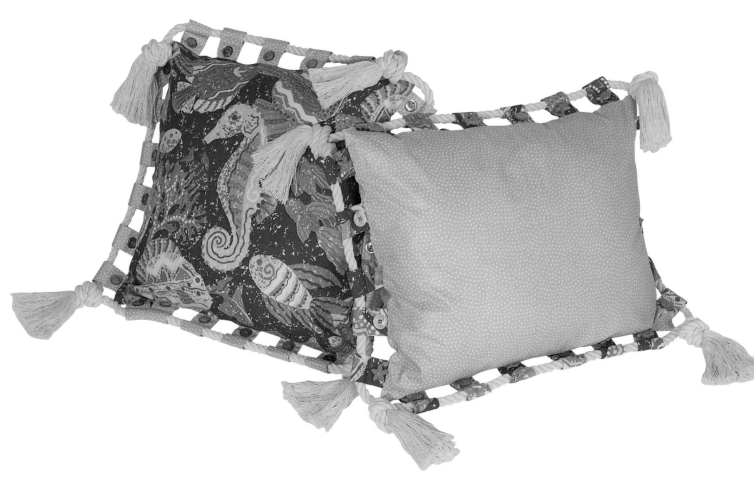

TABBED, CORDED
PILLOW COVER

Try this tabbed, knife-edge pillow cover as a fun alternative to any basic pillow design.
The type of cord threaded through the tabs makes this pillow casual or elegant.

1 From the pillow fabric, cut one 19" square for the pillow front (includes ½" seams all around). For the pillow back, cut one 9½" by 19" rectangle and one 14½" by 19" rectangle. From the tab fabric, cut three 4" strips the width of the fabric. Cut three 1" long pieces of hook-and-loop tape.

VOCABULARY

Tabs—extensions of fabric used as a method for hanging on curtain rods or dowels, or for threading cord.

Baste—to take long stitches either by machine or hand to hold pieces together temporarily before sewing the final seam.

TECHNIQUES YOU WILL LEARN

• Turning tubes • Basting

---

* Supplies are given for an 18"-square pillow cover

Fabric: ⅝ yard of decorator fabric

⅓ yard of coordinating decorator fabric for tabs

Notions: 4½ yards of ⅝"-wide cotton cord

⅛ yard of hook-and-loop tape

Matching sewing thread

Ruler, seam gauge, or tape measure

Needles: Universal needles #80/12

Other supplies: 18" pillow form

Masking tape

24 - ¾"-wide buttons (optional)

Large safety pin or Fasturn™ tube turning tool (optional)

T-pins (optional)

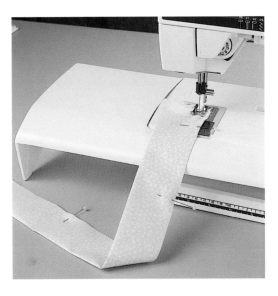

3 Fold the tab strips in half lengthwise with right sides together. Pin and sew the long side.

HANDY HINT

Begin pulling the tabs of fabric right side out through the tube turning tool with the seam allowance open. As the fabric tube is pulled through the tool, the seam allowance will be pressed open.

2 Fold the cotton cord into four equal lengths. Wrap masking tape around the cord to mark the lengths and cut the cord through the tape to prevent the cord from untwisting at each end.

continued

4 Turn the tubes of fabric right side out with a large safety pin or tube turning tool following the manufacturer's instructions. Press the seam to the center of the tubes. Cut 24 5½"-long tabs from the tubes.

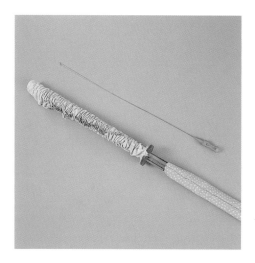

5 On one 19" side of each back fabric piece, press 2" to the wrong side. Open out the hem allowance and fold the cut edge into the crease making a double-fold 1" hem. Pin and topstitch the folded edge. Find the center of the smaller back fabric piece by folding the short sides together. Mark with a pin on the hemmed side.

HANDY HINT

Using your blindhem or edgestitch foot, guide the fabric along the raised edge of the foot, topstitching along the folded edge. Adjust your needle position as necessary to stitch close to the edge.

6 Lay the larger back fabric piece, wrong side up, on your tabletop. Separate the hook and loop sides of the 1" pieces from each other. Center the hook side of the tape over the pin in the hem allowance and pin. Pin the remaining two hook pieces 4" away from the center piece. Lay the small back fabric piece, right side up, opposite the larger piece and pin the loop pieces on the hem allowance to match with the hook tape on the larger back fabric piece. Topstitch the pieces in place on both back fabric pieces.

7 Fold the pillow front in quarters and mark the center of each side with a pin. Fold the tabs in half lengthwise with the seam inside. Pin a tab ¾" away from each side of the center creases. Pin the remaining tabs 1½" away so each side has six tabs; baste the tabs in place.

HANDY HINT

To quickly baste by machine, lengthen your stitch to 6.0 (longest length) and stitch. This stitch can be easily removed.

continued

8 Lay the small back fabric piece, wrong side down, on the tabletop. Overlap the large back fabric piece so the hook and loop sections stick together. Pin the pillow front, right sides together, over the pillow back. Stitch all four sides of the pillow cover. Trim the corners, turn right side out, and press.

HANDY HINT

For decorative detailing, sew buttons on the tabs between the pillow cover and the topstitching.

9 Topstitch through the tabs 1" from the edge of the pillow. Backstitch at the beginning and end of each line of stitching.

10 Thread the cotton cord through the tabs and tie knots at each corner. Remove the tape from the ends of the cord and unravel to make tassels. Trim the tassels to a 4" length.

HANDY HINT

Use T-pins to hold the cord taut between the corners while tying the knots.

PATCHWORK FLANGED
SHAM

Simple patchwork adds charm to the center of this easy-to-sew flanged pillow sham.

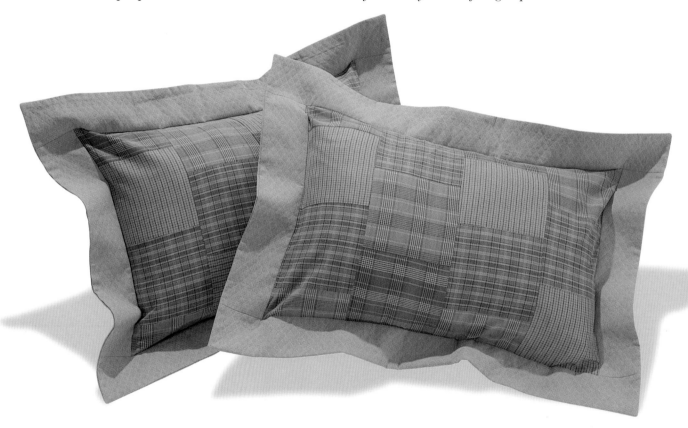

1 Measure the pillow length and width using a tape measure. Jot down the measurements.

HANDY HINT

A pre-quilted fabric like the one shown is the perfect choice for the flange and back fabric.

VOCABULARY

Clean-finish—to overcast the edges of the seam allowance with a zigzag, 3-step zigzag, or overcasting stitches or with the serger to prevent raveling.

Flange—a wide flat band often used on the edge of pillows.

Patchwork—also called piecing; sewing a variety of smaller pieces of fabric together to form a larger piece. In traditional piecing for quilt making, the pieces are usually sewn together with a ¼" seam allowance.

Selvedge—may also be spelled selvage, a tightly woven band on the lengthwise edge of the fabric.

"Stitch-in-the-ditch"—method of stitching in the groove of the seam through all thicknesses to hold the under layer in place.

TECHNIQUES YOU WILL LEARN

- Piecing fabrics
- Pressing
- Finishing raw edges
- "Stitch-in-the-ditch"

*All measurements are given for one standard-size pillow sham.

Fabric: ¼ yard of 44"/45"-wide assorted fabrics in three to four different prints
1 yard of 44"/45"-wide coordinating fabric for flange and back

Notions: Matching sewing thread
Fabric marking pen
Ruler or tape measure

Needles: Universal needles #80/12 or #90/14

Other supplies: Notepad and pencil
Cardboard

2 Before cutting your fabric, straighten the ends. Fold your fabric in half lengthwise and line up the selvedge edges; pin. Line up the cut ends with the markings on a cutting board or with the end of your table. If the edges are slanted, cut to straighten them.

3 To cut patchwork squares for the top, make a template from cardboard 6½" by 6¾". Trace the square onto your fabric, making sure to follow a straight grainline. Cut the patches along the markings. You will need a total of 12 squares.

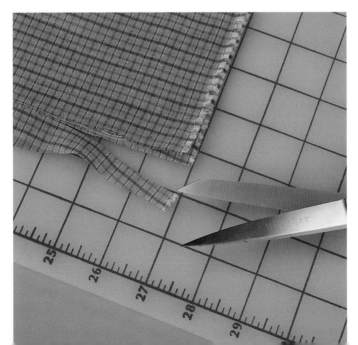

continued

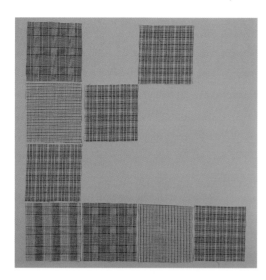

4 Lay the patches faceup on the table to determine your design pattern. Place four squares across and four down.

5 With right sides together, begin stitching the short (6½") sides of the patches together using a ¼" seam. Stitch the blocks to form strips with four squares in a row.

HANDY HINT

Many machines have a ¼" foot available for piecing. The standard seam allowance for piecing is ¼" wide.

6 Press the seam
allowance on all
squares to one side.

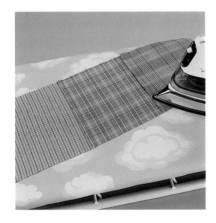

HANDY HINT

To clean-finish the
seams and avoid raveling
on the inside of the
sham top, cut a lining for
the top section 25" x
18" from muslin and
baste it to wrong side of
the patchwork top.
Continue as instructed.

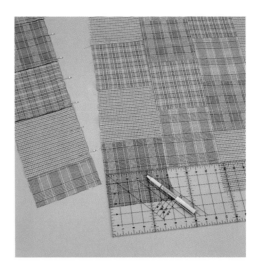

7 Join the pieced strips by
staggering the rows of patchwork
placing the first patch in the center of the
second row. Continue joining the strips
staggering them row by row to form the
sham top. Cut the finished patchwork top
to measure 25" by 18".

8 Cut two flange strips for the top
and bottom, 32" by 4" and two
side pieces, 19" by 4". Cut two back
pieces, 20½" by 25". Be sure to
straighten your fabric before cutting.

9 To clean-finish the sham's back
edges, use 3-step zigzag stitch with
your overcast foot. Align cut edge with
the guide on the foot and stitch around all
edges of each back section.

continued

HANDY HINT

Place a piece of masking tape on the bed of your machine 2½" from the needle and use as a stitching guide.

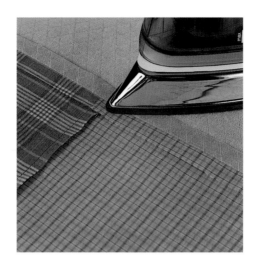

10 With right sides together, stitch the side flange pieces to the 18" edge of the patchwork top using a ½" seam allowance. Press the seam open. Stitch the top and bottom flanges to the patchwork top. Press the seam open.

11 Press under 3" on each short edge of the back pieces. Topstitch 2½" from pressed edges.

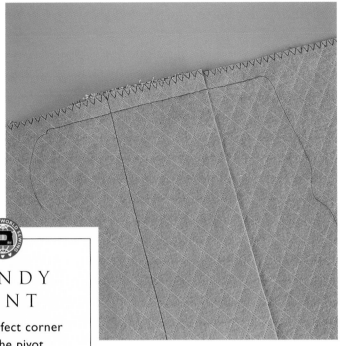

HANDY HINT

For the perfect corner point, use the pivot method when stitching. Stop the machine when you come to within $1/2$" from the end or corner. Use the handwheel to place your needle into the fabric. Raise the presser foot with the needle still in the fabric. Pivot the fabric 90 degrees into position, lower the presser foot, and continue stitching.

12 Place the back pieces face up on a table and overlap the topstitched edges 4"; pin. Baste the edges together to hold in place.

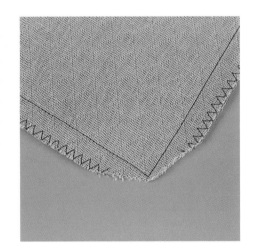

13 With right sides together and the edges even, pin the back section to the top. Stitch using a $1/2$" seam allowance. Cut across the corners to eliminate any bulk. Cut off any excess seam allowance at the corner point and at each side. Turn the pillow sham right side out and press.

14 Working from the top of the pillow sham, pin through all the layers along the seam where the flange meets the patchwork. Using a blindhem or edgestitch foot, "stitch-in-the-ditch" or groove of the seam through all the thicknesses. You may have to move the needle position for stitching accuracy.

TIED
PILLOWS

Learn to mix fabrics for interesting effects on this elegantly tied pillow.

VOCABULARY

Chair tie—Tassels linked by straight length of twisted cord (approximately 27").
Cutting line—marked line on which to cut out fabric.
Overlay—piece of fabric or lace placed on top of another for decorative purposes.

TECHNIQUES YOU WILL LEARN

- Mixing fabrics
- Adding decorative cording
- Trimming
- Slipstitching

*All measurements are given for an 18" pillow.
Fabric: 1 yard of decorator fabric
    1 yard of contrasting fabric for overlay
Notions: 1½ yards of ½" twisted cord with lip
    1 yard of ¼" twisted cord with lip
    One chair tie with tassels
    Matching sewing thread
    Fabric marking pen
    Ruler or tape measure
Needles: Universal needles #80/12
Other supplies: 18"-square pillow form

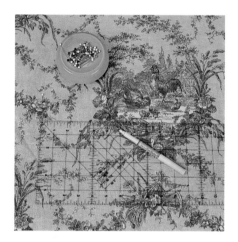

1 Print fabrics with large motifs will need to be centered on the pillow. Before cutting, find the center of the design; pin-mark. Measure out 9½" from side to side and top to bottom for a 19" square. Mark the cutting line with a fabric marking pen and ruler. Do the same for the pillow back. Cut out following the marked lines. Cut two 19" squares of contrasting fabric for the overlay.

2 Pin the ¼" twisted cord to two opposite edges of one of the overlay sections and baste in place using a zipper foot positioned to the right of the needle.

3 With right sides together, pin the remaining overlay section to the corded overlay piece along the corded edges. Stitch the pinned edges with the corded section on top using a zipper foot and moving the needle position slightly to the left up against the cord. Turn the overlay section right side out and press.

HANDY HINT

Position the zipper foot up against the cord. Move the needle as close to the cord as possible without hitting the foot. You will get a stitching line very close to the cord or use an extra accessory, the piping tool, to apply the cord and stitch the seam. The cord rides in the groove on the bottom of the foot.

continued

4 Place the overlay section on top of the right side of one pillow piece. Machine-baste the cut edges to pillow piece.

5 Pin the ½" twisted cord to the right side of the remaining pillow piece along the edge so that the cord faces the inside of the pillow and the lip is even with the cut edges. Overlap the cut edges and trim the excess cord. Using a zipper foot positioned on the right side of the needle, baste the cord to the fabric. To square the cord around the corner, clip the cord lip up to the cording and at each side of the corner to help it lie flat.

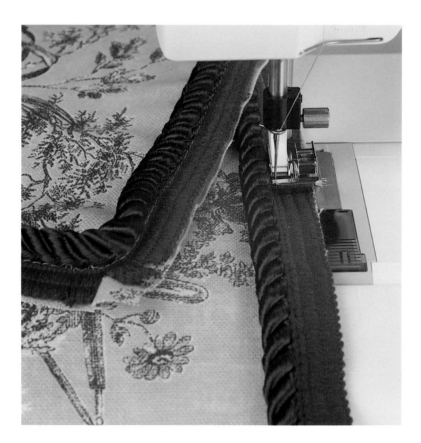

HANDY HINT

To square the corner, leave the needle down in the fabric, pivot 45°, and take two stitches across the corner. Leaving the needle down, pivot 45° again and continue sewing. Repeat at each corner.

6 Pin the pillow front to the back with right sides together and the corded side up. Using a zipper foot, move the needle just inside the line of basting to crowd the stitching against the cording. Stitch, leaving an 8" opening on one side for turning and stuffing.

HANDY HINT

Braided or twisted cord can be joined neatly at the ends by twisting the individual cords together. Starting at the center on one edge of the pillow square, stitch the cording leaving 2" of cord free at the beginning. End stitching 1" from center. Remove the lip from the cord

ends up to the stitching by pulling the thread chain. Gently untwist the ends of the cord and wrap each end with transparent tape to secure. Begin twisting the ends together into one continuous line of cording. Hold the newly twisted cord in place with transparent tape or pins. Baste along the lip of the cord in the same direction as the braid twists. Trim the cord and flatten along the seam.

7 Cut across the corners to eliminate bulk and turn the pillow right side out. Press. Insert the pillow form and slipstitch the opening closed. Wrap the chair tie around the center of the overlay and tie.

KID'S LOUNGE-LEOPARD
PILLOW

*These over-sized pillows are perfect for lounging in front of
the TV or the privacy of your bedroom.*

VOCABULARY

Covered cord—often referred to as piping, fabric-
covered cord is used as trim on pillows, cushions,
and upholstered pieces as well as on the edge of
collars, cuffs, or other garments. Filler cable cord is
wrapped with a bias strip of fabric leaving a narrow
edge of fabric to be stitched into the seam
allowance.

TECHNIQUES
YOU WILL LEARN

- Measuring a pillow
- Adding piping to a seam
- Turning corners with trims

*Supplies are given for a 30"-square pillow.
Fabric: 2 yards of decorator fabric
Notions: 3$^1/_2$ yards of covered cord with lip
  Matching sewing thread
  Tape measure
Needles: Universal needles #80/12
Other supplies: 30"-square pillow form
  Four decorative tassels (optional)

1 Measure the length and width of the
pillow form from seam to seam and
add a ½" seam allowance on all sides.
(For example: Cut two 31" squares for
a 30"-square pillow.)

2 Pin the covered cord to the right side of one fabric square matching the edges so the covered cord is toward the inside of the pillow. Using a zipper foot positioned on the right side of the needle, baste the covered cord to the fabric square. Stop stitching approximately ½" from the corner and cut the cording lip up to the filler cord to ease the cording around the corner and help it lie flat. Continue stitching, repeating this procedure at each corner. (See Handy Hint, page 52.)

3 At the end, remove 1" of stitching from each end of the cording. Trim the filler cord so the ends just meet. Fold under ½" of the cording fabric on one end and wrap it around the other end. Continue stitching, backstitching at the end to hold.

continued

DESIGN ✿ OPTIONS

Add decorative tassels to the pillow corners. From the right side of the fabric square, pin or hand-tack the tassels in each corner placing the tassel cord across the seamline and the tassel strands lying toward the center. Stitch tassel cord in place when stitching the seam. Tassels can be added to the pillow corners with or without the covered cord trim.

4 With right sides together, pin the remaining fabric piece to the corded piece. Using a zipper foot, place the fabric under the presser foot with the corded section on top. Move the needle just inside the line of basting to crowd the stitching against the cording. Stitch, leaving an 18" opening for turning and stuffing.

5 Cut across the corners to eliminate any bulk. Turn the pillow cover right side out and press.

6 Insert the pillow form and slip-stitch the opening closed.

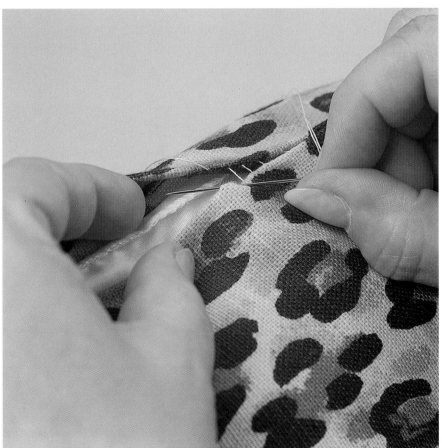

HANDY HINT

If the cording is omitted from the edge of the pillow, use your standard presser foot when stitching the front fabric square to the back.

EASY BISTRO
CHAIR COVER

Cover any straight-backed chair with this very easy chair cover-up. It's a simple solution for sprucing up a room for any party in no time at all.

VOCABULARY

Lining—fabric used on the reverse side to provide stability to a project; the lining can often be seen so the same fabric or an equally as nice a fabric is used for lining.

TECHNIQUES YOU WILL LEARN

- Measuring a chair
- Matching striped fabric
- Making ties from bias tape

Fabric: Decorator fabric — yardage based on size of chair
Notions: Grided pattern tracing paper
   Package of wide bias tape
   Matching sewing thread
   Ruler, seam gauge, and flexible tape measure
   Fabric marking pen
Needles: Universal needles #80/12
Other supplies: Notepaper
   Pen

1 Measure the height of the back of the chair and mark the measurement down on paper adding 1" for seams. Measure the depth of the seat, the height from the floor to the seat and from the seat to the top of the back; jot this combined measurement down adding 1" for seams. Measure the width of the chair at its widest point adding 1" and jot this down. Cut two pieces of pattern tracing paper according to the width and length dimensions you took. Pin the narrow edges together with a ½" seam allowance and place on chair to check your measurements. Make adjustments as necessary.

HANDY HINT

When measuring the width of your chair, take into consideration any curving of the back and allow for that in your measurement. Otherwise your cover won't be wide enough.

2 Cut two pieces for the front and two pieces for the back from your patterns. One set of pieces will be used for the lining.

HANDY HINT

By making this chair cover in two pieces, the seam at the top edge of the chair back helps hold the cover in place and eliminates a lot of slipping.

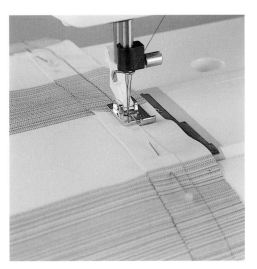

3 Along the narrower edge of the back piece, press in a ½" seam allowance. Place this piece, right sides together, on top of the front piece ½" away from the edge matching the stripes. Carefully pin the pieces together. Stitch, using your blindhem or edgestitch foot, very close to the pressed edge producing perfectly matched seams. Open out your seam and press. Repeat this procedure on the remaining lining pieces.

continued

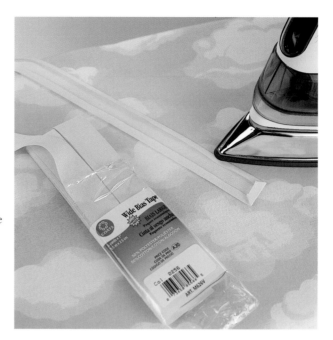

4 Cut eight 12"-long pieces of wide bias tape. Trim the corners of one end, fold in ¼", and press.

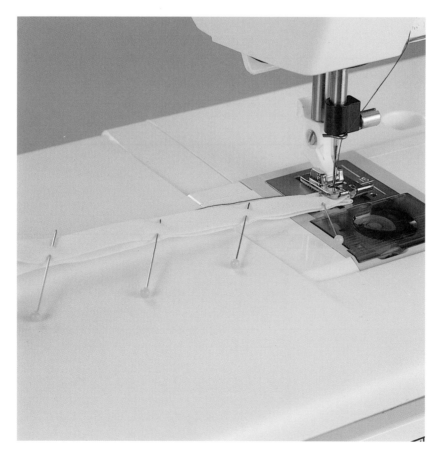

5 Fold the strips in half lengthwise, wrong sides together, and pin. Stitch across the end and up the sides.

6 Place the chair cover over the chair with the seam at the top of the back. Mark the tie placement at the point where the seat connects with the back and approximately 6" above that on both sides. Pin one tie at each mark on the right side. Baste the ties in place.

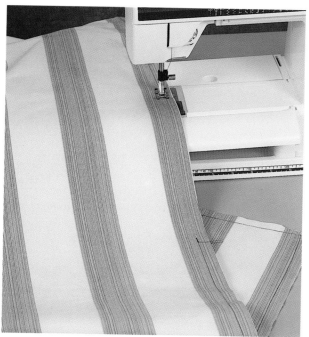

7 Pin the lining piece to the outer piece and stitch using a ½" seam allowance leaving a 6" opening for turning. Trim the corners, turn to the right side, and press. Slipstitch the opening closed by hand or edgestitch around all the edges by machine.

8 Position the cover on the chair and tie the sides together to hold in place.

Round Boxed
PILLOW

Stitch up a round boxed pillow as an interesting variation
to the basic square pillow.

VOCABULARY

Boxed pillow—additional banding added between pillow top and bottom forming a boxed shape; pillows can be round, square, rectangular, or other unique shapes (e.g. stars, triangles, etc.).

TECHNIQUES
YOU WILL LEARN

- Covering buttons
- Making a boxing band

Fabric: Decorator fabric — yardage based on size of pillow
Notions: Cording with a lip — yardage based on size of pillow
2"-thick polyurethane foam square for pillow form
Two 1½" buttons to cover
Fabric marking pen
Tape measure
Matching sewing thread
Needles: Universal needles #80/12
Other supplies: Hand-sewing needle
Upholstery needle
Felt tip marker
Serrated or electric knife
Polyester batting (optional)

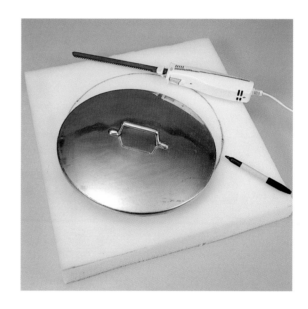

1 Using a felt tip marker, trace a round object of the desired circumference (a pot lid or something similar) onto the foam. Cut the foam along the marking using an electric or serrated knife.

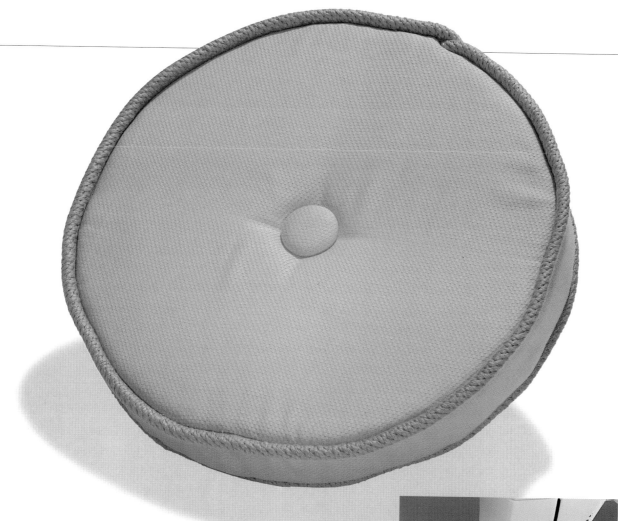

2 On the wrong side of your fabric, trace the circle using a fabric marking pen and add ½" around the circumference for the seam allowance. Cut two circles of fabric.

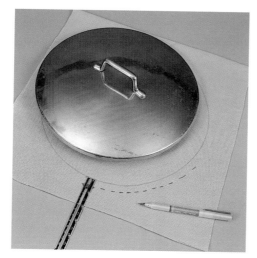

3 Pin the cording to the edges of both circles overlapping the ends and baste in place using a zipper foot positioned to the right of the needle. Clip the seam allowance and the cording lip at intervals to ease around the curve.

continued

63

4 Measure around the circumference of the pillow form using a flexible tape measure. Cut a 3"-wide boxing strip the pillow circumference plus 1". Stitch the short ends of the band, right sides together, using a ½" seam. Press the seam open.

5 Pin the boxing strip to one circle matching the raw edges. Stitch using a zipper foot, moving the needle as close to the right to crowd the cord. Pin the remaining circle section to the other edge of the strip and stitch leaving an opening to insert the pillow form.

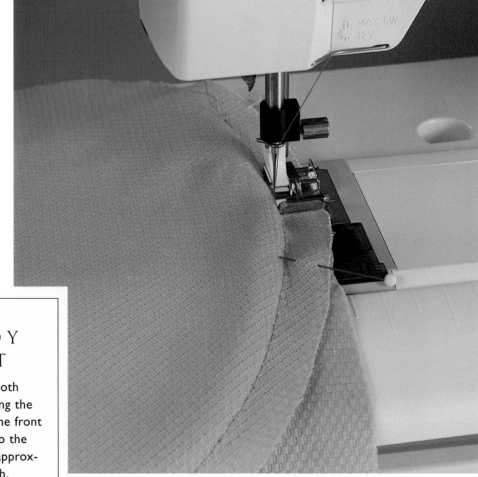

HANDY HINT

To achieve a smooth curve when sewing the boxing band to the front and back, clip into the seam allowance approximately every inch.

6 Turn the pillow cover right side out and press. Insert the pillow form and slipstitch the opening closed.

HANDY HINT

To soften the edges of the foam insert, cut two layers of polyester batting for the top, bottom, and band. Wrap the batting around the foam and loosely hand-stitch together before inserting into the fabric cover.

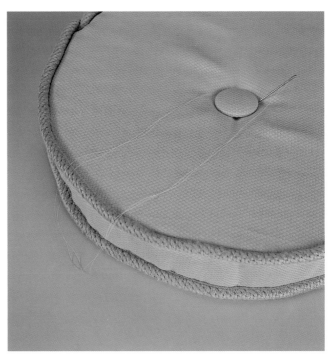

8 Using an upholstery needle and thread, tie the end of the thread to the shank of the button, leaving a 4" tail. Insert the needle through the center of the pillow and pull tight. Thread the needle through the second button and bring it tight against the opposite side of the pillow. Wrap the thread around the button shank and tie off the thread ends.

7 Following the manufacturer's instructions, cover two large buttons with the pillow fabric.

SIMPLE CHAIR
CHAIR COVER
AND
SEAT CUSHION

*Expand your seating arrangement and quickly change the look of the
room by covering the back and adding a seat cushion to a simple kitchen chair.*

VOCABULARY

Brush fringe—ornamental trim with loose
strands of thread, yarn, or beads attached to a
woven band.

Fuse—to adhere interfacing or fleece to a fabric
generally by heat from an iron and pressure. It is
best to follow the manufacturer's directions for
each fusing product.

Twisted cord—decorative trim used on edges of
pillows, cushions, upholstery, and clothing. Decorative threads are wrapped together forming cord
with or without a lip attached.

TECHNIQUES
YOU WILL LEARN

- Working with a commercial pattern
- Adding brush trim
- Making a pattern

Fabric: Decorator fabric — yardage based on size
  of chair
  Lining fabric for facing — yardage based on size
  of chair

Notions: Commercial pattern if available (e.g.
  Simplicity #7966)
  Grided pattern tracing paper
  Fabric marking pen
  Matching sewing thread
  Tape measure
  Twisted cord with lip, yardage based on size of
  chair
  Brush fringe for bottom of chair back cover, sides
  and front of chair seat cover, yardage based on
  size of chair

Needles: Universal needles #80/12 #90/14

Other supplies: Two pieces of fusible fleece for
  chair back and two pieces for chair seat —
  yardage based on size of chair
  Removable masking tape
  Iron

1 Select a commercial pattern of your choice. Trim the pattern pieces necessary for the chair back and seat cushion. Tape the back pattern piece to the chair and place the seat cushion on the seat to measure the size for fit. For an unusual or oversized chair, it will be necessary to make a pattern of your own.

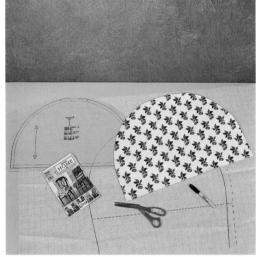

3 Add 1" for ease and the seam allowance to the top curved edge and ½" seam allowance across the bottom straight edge. Cut two pieces from the decorator fabric, two pieces from the lining fabric, and two pieces from the fusible fleece for each chair back.

HANDY HINT

Even if you make a pattern for yourself, you can still follow the instructions for sewing that come with the commercial pattern.

continued

4 First, fuse or baste one piece of fleece to the wrong side of each back fabric piece. Trim the fused or basted fleece close to the seamline.

5 Pin and, using the zipper foot, baste the twisted cord to the outer curved edge of the other back fabric piece. Fold the ends of the cord toward the raw edge ¼" from the bottom edge.

HANDY HINT

You may need to skip steps in the commercial instructions dealing with decorative details you are not using on your pattern, such as ruffles or other trims.

6 With right sides together, pin the front to the back. Using a zipper foot, stitch the long curved seam, stitching through the cord as it crosses the seamline at each end.

7 With right sides together, pin the back lining pieces along the outer curved edge. Stitch, leaving an opening about 5" at the center of the curved seam for turning.

8 Pin the lining to the back section, right sides together, along the lower edges, matching the seams. Stitch along the pinned edge and turn to the right side through the opening in the lining. Slipstitch the opening closed. Press.

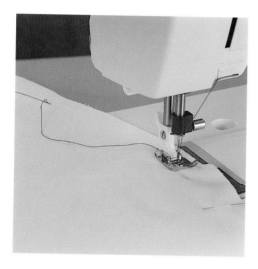

9 Pin the brush fringe to the right side along the lower edge of the chair cover, ¼" from the edge, starting and stopping at the center back leaving a 1" overlap. Carefully unravel just enough fringe at each end until the fringe ends butt firmly against each other. Top-stitch the fringe in place. Unravel the basting thread from the bottom of the fringe.

continued

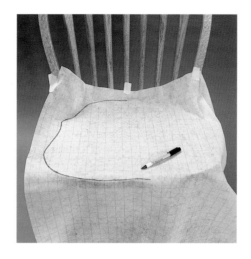

10 For the seat cushion, tape the pattern tracing paper to the seat of the chair and trace around the edge. Mark the placement for the chair seat ties with dots. Add 1" to front and side edges for ease and seam allowance, and ½" to the back of the chair seat for the seam allowance.

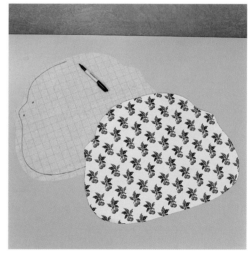

11 Cut two pieces of fabric and two pieces of fleece for each seat cushion. Cut four, 14" by 4", strips for each chair. Fuse or baste the fleece to the wrong sides of each fabric piece. Trim the fleece close to the seamline.

HANDY HINT

The Fasturn™ tool makes turning tubes easy. This tool is available in a variety of sizes.

12 Fold each tie strip, wrong sides together, and stitch along one long edge and one short edge using a ½" seam allowance. Trim the corners and seam allowance to ¼". Turn and press.

HANDY HINT

It may be necessary to adjust the placement of the ties so they will easily surround the chair back supports.

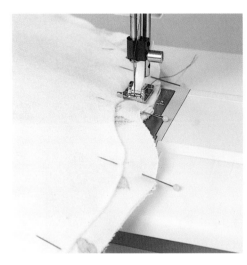

14 Pin the two seat sections, right sides together. Stitch around the edge with a ½" seam allowance leaving a 5" opening at the center back for turning. Turn and press. Slipstitch the opening closed.

13 Pin two ties to each corner on the back edge of one fabric section at the dots, matching the raw edges. Baste in place.

15 Pin the brush fringe ¼" from the outside edge of the seat cushion at the front and sides. Topstitch in place. Remove the basting thread at the lower edge of the brush fringe.

CHILD'S
CHAIR COVER

Make these wonderful chair covers for any child-size chair.

Add their name and decorative buttons to the back.

VOCABULARY

Pattern Tracing Paper—fabric-type material or paper used for pattern making; usually grided with 1" squares.

Staystitch—a reinforcing stitch usually stitched 1/8" inside the seamline to control stretching on curves and in corners.

TECHNIQUES
YOU WILL LEARN

• Making a pattern
• Making more than one buttonhole the same size
• Sewing on buttons by machine

Fabric: 1¹/₂ yards of 60"-wide decorator fabric

Notions: 1¹/₂ yards of grided pattern tracing paper
¹/₈ yard of fusible woven interfacing
Matching sewing thread
Fabric marking pen
40 wt. rayon embroidery thread (optional)

Needles: Universal needles #80/12 or #90/14 (the size depends on the weight of the fabric)

Other supplies: Child-size chair
Tear-away stabilizer (optional)
Permanent fabric marking pen (optional)

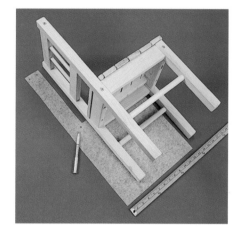

1 Lay the SIDE of the chair on a single layer of pattern tracing paper and trace the outline. Remove the chair and draw a line connecting the bottom edge of the chair legs. On the pattern tracing paper, draw a 1" hem allowance outside the bottom line and ½" seam allowances to the remaining sides. Make dots on the pattern ½" inside the corners to mark the chair back and seat.

2 Cut a BUTTON EXTENSION pattern piece 5" wide by the length of the SIDE piece minus ½".

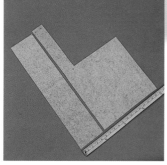

HANDY HINT

Use grided pattern tracing paper for your pattern making. The paper is blocked with 1" squares which makes adding seam allowances and hems very easy. When drawing a pattern, the lines can be used to mark the grainline of fabric also.

3 Lay the chair front on a single layer of pattern tracing paper. For the SKIRT FRONT pattern, trace the width of the seat and height of the legs. Remove the chair and draw a line to connect the bottom edge of the chair legs. Draw a 1" hem allowance outside the bottom line on the pattern piece and ½" seam allowances to the other sides.

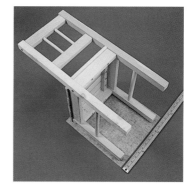

4 For the BACK, FRONT, and SEAT pattern pieces, begin by laying the back of the chair on the pattern tracing paper and tracing the outline. Allow enough pattern tracing paper to wrap over the top, down the front, and across the seat. Draw a line to connect the bottom edge of the legs. Add a 1" hem allowance to the bottom side of the pattern. To either side of the outline of the chair back, add 2" for a facing.

continued

D E S I G N ✿ O P T I O N S

Prior to stitching any fabric pieces together, add your child's name to the center back of the BACK, FRONT, and SEAT piece with embroidery or a permanent fabric marking pen. You can add easy appliqués or other design elements, too.

6 On the front of the chair, measure from the top of the chair to the seat. Extend the BACK, FRONT, and SEAT pattern by this measurement and draw a line. Measure from the chair back to the front edge of the seat. Extend the pattern by this measurement and draw a line. Measure the width of the seat edge and mark on the pattern. Connect the side outline of the chair back to the width of the seat edge. Add ½" to all the sides of the seat, the back, and top of 2" facing. Make dots ½" inside the pattern edge on each line, marking the position of each edge.

5 Measure the depth of the top of the chair. Extend the BACK, FRONT, and SEAT pattern at the top by the depth and draw a line.

7 Using the newly drawn pattern pieces, cut two SIDES, one BUTTON EXTENSION, one SKIRT FRONT, and one BACK, FRONT, and SEAT for each chair. Transfer all dots to the wrong side of the fabric with a fabric marking pen. Cut a piece of interfacing 2" wide and equal to the length of the chair back.

8 Fuse the interfacing to the wrong side of the BACK, FRONT, and SEAT side with the facing. Position the interfacing 2" from the cut edge. Finish the edge of the facing with a three-step zigzag or any other overcast stitch.

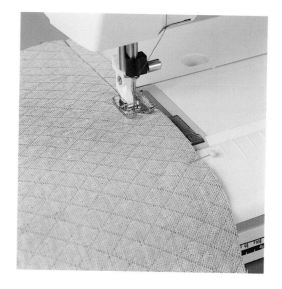

HANDY HINT

The 3-step zigzag stitches its way from side to side on the edge of the fabric. Sew this stitch using a special overcast foot to keep the edge of the fabric from being drawn up.

9 Sew the SKIRT FRONT to the BACK, FRONT, and SEAT piece at the seat front. Press the seam allowances toward the lower seat.

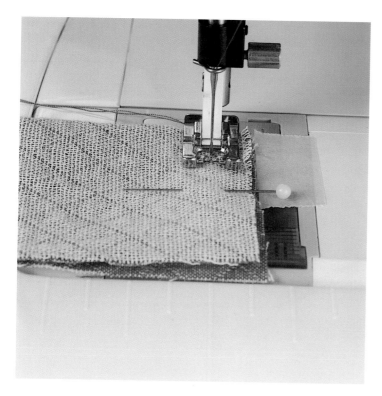

10 Fold the BUTTON EXTENSION in half lengthwise with right sides together. Sew both short ends. Turn the extension right side out and press.

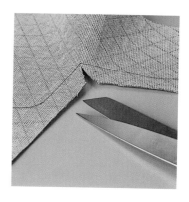

11 Staystitch the inside corners of the SIDE pieces and clip into the seam allowances to the stitching line.

continued

12 Pin the SIDES to the BACK, FRONT, and SEAT with right sides together, matching the dots and sew the pieces together. On the side of the seat with the facing, begin the seam at the dot near the top of the facing and continue to the hem. Press the seam allowances to one side. Press 2" of facing toward the inside of the chair cover.

13 Pin the BUTTON EXTENSION to the remaining open SIDE of the chair cover back. The BUTTON EXTENSION will be 1" shorter than the SIDE. Seam the pieces together and press the seam allowance in one direction.

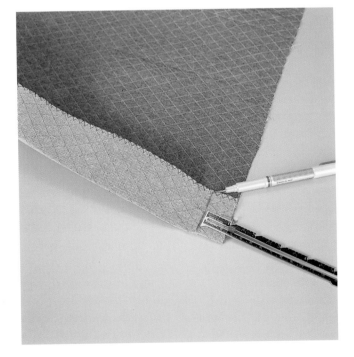

14 Fold the facing toward the right side of the fabric and pin. Draw a stitching line 1" from the raw edge. Sew on the line. Trim the corner and turn to the right side. Press the seam.

16 Sew five buttonholes on the faced edge of the BACK, FRONT, and SEAT. Mark the first buttonhole 2½" from the top of the facing and ½" away from the finished edge. Space the other buttonholes 4" apart. Use a button to mark the length of the buttonhole, or select the size of the button on your sewing machine and use the sensor buttonhole foot to automatically make each buttonhole the correct size. Sew the buttonholes. Dot seam sealant in between the bars of stitching. Allow to dry. Use a buttonhole knife or seam ripper to cut open.

15 Pin up a 1" hem around the bottom edge of the chair cover. Fold the hem allowance like an "S" and sew the hem with the blindhem stitch.

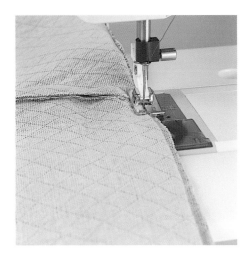

17 Lay the buttonholes over the BUTTON EXTENSION. Mark the placement for the buttons on the BUTTON EXTENSION. Mark the placement for decorative buttons on the opposite side of the BACK, FRONT, and SEAT 2½" from the top and 1" from the edge. Space the other buttons 4" apart. Sew on the buttons by hand or machine.

PLACE MATS & TABLE COVERS

REVERSIBLE QUILTED
PLACE MATS AND NAPKINS

Quick-and-easy reversible, quilted place mats perform dual duty on any table. Matching hemmed napkins provide the finishing touch.

VOCABULARY

Channel quilting—to stitch with parallel straight lines through all layers of fabric and batting creating a quilted effect.

Miter—to form a square corner by stitching the fabrics on a diagonal.

TECHNIQUES YOU WILL LEARN

• Channel quilting
• Methods of basting
• Mitered corners

*Supplies given are for 18" by 14" finished place mat and 22" square napkins

Fabric: 2 yards of decorator or quilting fabric for four place mats or 1 yard each of two coordinating prints

1¹/₂ yards of fabric for four napkins

1 yard of cotton batting such as Quilter's Dream for place mats

Notions: Matching sewing thread
Ruler or yardstick
Fabric marking pen
Quilt pins

Needles: Universal needles #80/12 or #90/14

Other supplies: Dual feed foot
Quilting Bar
Fabric chalk
Edgestitching foot

1 Cut eight rectangles of place
mat fabric, 19" by 15". Cut
four batting rectangles, 19" by 15".

2 Place two fabric rectangles right sides together.
Layer one piece of batting on the wrong side
of the top fabric. Pin all the layers together.

3 Stitch around the outer edges using
½" seams leaving an opening for
turning. Trim across the corners and trim
the batting to ¼" from the seam.

continued

4 Turn each place mat right side out. Press lightly. Slipstitch the opening closed.

HANDY HINT

Many sewing machines have built-in basting stitches or use your machine's longest stitch length. Check your instruction manual for information. Or take long running stitches by hand pulling the stitches slightly snug to securely hold all the layers together. Do not make knots in the thread ends.

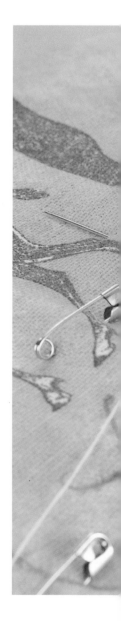

5 To prevent the layers from shifting, machine, pin, or hand-baste the layers together. Begin by pin basting, starting from the center of the place mat and working to the edges, spacing safety pins in rows approximately 1"-2" apart. Machine-baste by stitching across the place mat using a long stitch length and a dual feed foot.

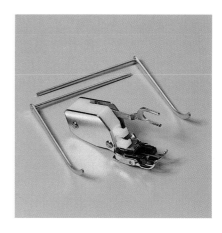

6 To channel-quilt the place mat, first attach a quilting bar (if available) to the presser foot and use a dual feed foot. Using a ruler and fabric marking pen, draw a diagonal line from one corner to the opposite side. Stitch along the marking using a slightly longer stitch length.

HANDY HINT

A dual-feed foot is a very valuable presser foot to own. The action of the feed dogs on the foot work together with the machine feed teeth to keep the layers from sliding. It is used for quilting, when sewing slippery fabrics such as velvet or velveteen, or when matching plaids and stripes to keep all the layers together.

continued

7 Adjust your quilting bar 1½" away from your sewing machine needle. Place the quilting bar on the previous line of stitching and continue stitching in straight parallel rows covering the entire place mat.

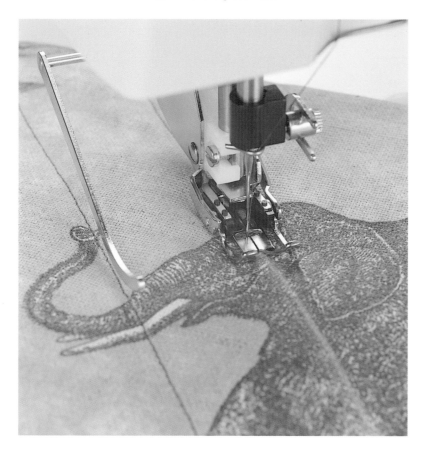

HANDY HINT

If you do not have a quilting bar, use transparent tape or fabric chalk to mark the quilting lines. Guide the edge of the presser foot next to the tape or chalk line as you sew.

8 Cut four 23" squares for the napkins. Press under ½" along all outer edges. Press under 1" again along all outer edges.

HANDY HINT

Create unique quilting effects by using decorative machine stitches in place of a straight stitch.

9 To miter the corners, open out the pressed edges. Fold each corner diagonally with right sides together and matching two side edges. Using a fabric marking pen and ruler, mark from the fold to the pressed marking on the diagonal.

10 Stitch along the markings. Trim the seam allowance leaving ⅜". Turn right side out, folding under the pressed edge.

11 Stitch close to the inside fold to hem each napkin using your blindhem or edgestitch foot. Press when complete.

TRIMMED
PLACE MATS AND NAPKINS

Add a little lace to the edges of
simple-to-sew place mats and napkins for a trendy look.

1 Cut two pieces from the decorator fabric, 19" by 15" for each place mat. Place two pieces, right sides together, with a piece of cotton batting on top. Pin all layers together. Stitch along all four sides leaving a 5" opening to turn in the middle of one short side.

VOCABULARY

Batting—filling used as stuffing; can be made from cotton, wool, fiberfil, silk, or other materials.

Cluny lace—a coarse bobbin lace either made by hand or machine.

TECHNIQUES YOU WILL LEARN

- Mock mitering lace at corners

*Supplies given for a set of four place mats and napkins

Fabric: 1½ yards of decorator fabric for place mats
1 yard of 52"-wide decorator fabric for napkins

Notions: 19" x 15" lightweight cotton batting for each place mat
2 yards of flat 1" Cluny lace for each place mat
2 yards of flat 1" Cluny lace for each napkin
Air- or water-soluble marking pen
Matching sewing thread
Ruler

Needles: Universal needles #80/12

2 Trim the batting close to the stitching. Clip the corners, turn, and press.

3 Select a pattern line in the fabric, or mark, with an air- or water-soluble marking pen, straight lines 1" apart across the short and long sides of each place mat. Set the stitch length to 3mm and machine-quilt following the marked lines.

HANDY HINT

Reduce your presser foot pressure instead of using a dual feed foot to help the fabric layers from shifting.

continued

4 Beginning 2" from the end of the lace, pin the flat lace to the place mat edge starting at a corner. To turn the corners with a "mock" miter, extend the lace 1" beyond the corner, then fold the lace at a 45-degree angle from the corner. Pin the miter in place and continue around all four sides of the place mat, folding at each corner.

HANDY HINT

You can use a flat or pre-gathered lace for your edging trim.

5 To finish, pin the lace all the way to the corner. Fold the lace at a 45-degree angle and then in line with the extended edge of lace. Stitch along the lace edge on all four sides. Press. Straight-stitch across the mitered edges at each corner.

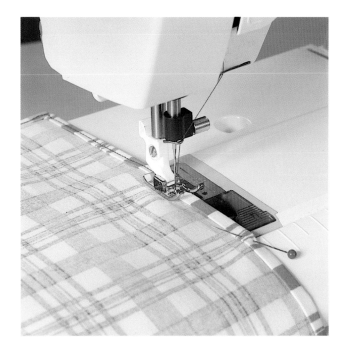

6 Cut a 17" square of decorator fabric for each napkin. Press under a ¼" double-fold hem at each side of the napkin. Topstitch ⅛" from the folded edge.

7 Pin the lace to the top of the napkin and stitch in place over the previous line of stitching, mitering the corners of lace in same manner as for the place mats.

HANDY HINT

Check the remnant table at your fabric store for small pieces of elegant fabrics. Since these pieces are usually short lengths, they are often reduced in price.

1 Cut one 15" by 45" rectangle from muslin. Fold the piece in half lengthwise and place a mark 5" from the end along the raw edges. Draw a line from the mark to the center fold; cut the ends to a point.

CRAZY PATCH

TABLE RUNNER

Mix and match elegant fabrics for this beautiful tabletop

runner. Since there is no real pattern to follow, you can design your own!

90

VOCABULARY

Crazy patch—to piece a variety of fabric types and shapes together; embroidery is often used as topical embellishment.

Velvet board—board covered with pin points used for pressing napped fabrics.

TECHNIQUES YOU WILL LEARN

- Sewing more difficult fabrics
- Sewing decorative stitches
- Pressing velvets, velveteen
- Adding tassels into seams

*Supplies are given for a finished 12" by 42" table runner

Fabric: ¼ yard of four to five assorted colors of velvets, velveteen, brocades, or chenille

1¼ yards of muslin

⅜ yard of lining fabric

Notions: Two tassels

Matching sewing thread

Fabric marking pen

Rayon and metallic threads (optional)

Needles: Universal needles #80/12

Embroidery or metallic needles #80/12 for decorative threads

Other supplies: Tear-away stabilizer (optional)

2 Cut two 13" by 22" rectangles from the lining.

3 Choose one fabric from the assortment of fabrics for a center patch. Cut a multi-sided piece that is approximately 7". Pin the patch, wrong side down, near the center of the muslin rectangle. Sew around the patch with a straight stitch.

HANDY HINT

Use the edge of the presser foot along the edge of the fabric when stitching down the pieces to reduce bulk.

continued

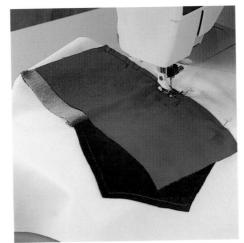

4 Use other fabrics to frame the multi-sided patch using the "flip and sew" method by laying the next piece of fabric, right sides together, on top of the multi-sided patch. Matching the raw edges, pin the fabric along one side and sew.

5 Flip open the newly sewn piece toward the muslin. Finger-press the seam. Each time a new patch is added, with right sides together, cover the raw edges of the previous patch and choose a new angle for the seamline. Continue to randomly piece fabrics working out from the center patch covering the entire muslin foundation. The edges of the decorative fabric may extend beyond the muslin edges.

6 Using a decorative presser foot, sew decorative stitches with rayon and metallic threads over the seams to highlight the crazy patch piecing. Add monograms or other embellishments of your choice to the top.

7 Trim the pieced table runner top to 13" by 43". With the right sides of the lining pieces together, pin one short side and sew a ½" seam leaving 5" opening in the center for turning. Press the seam allowance open.

9 With right sides together, pin the table runner top and lining together. Trim away any excess lining at the pointed ends. Sew around the outside edges of the table runner. Trim the corners.

8 Pin one tassel to the right side at each point of the runners with the tassel to the inside.

10 Turn right side out through the opening in the lining. Lightly press the edges from the lining side. Slipstitch the opening in the lining closed.

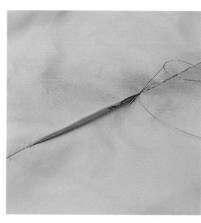

HANDY HINT

Press velvets, velveteen, or other fabrics with nap carefully to avoid any shiny iron marks. Place the fabric face down on a terry cloth towel or a velvet board and steam press lightly.

FITTED ROUND
TABLECLOTH

*Add an elegant touch to a lamp or small side table with this
sheer fitted cloth. The ribbon trim completes the look.*

VOCABULARY

Clean-finish the edge—prevent the fabric edge
from raveling by using a zigzag or a serger stitch to
overcast.
Double-fold hem—to fold up the edge of the
fabric twice by the same amount; hem can be
finished with a blindhem or edgestitched.
Edgestitch—to stich very close to the finished or
folded edge as on hems, collars, or cuffs.

TECHNIQUES
YOU WILL LEARN

- Gathering over cord
- Hemming sheer fabrics
- Attaching ribbon

Fabric: Sheer decorator fabric such as chiffon —
  yardage based on measurement of table
Notions: 5/8"-wide satin ribbon — yardage based on
    width of skirt
  Gimp cord or string
  Matching sewing thread
  Tape measure or ruler
  Fabric marking pen
Needles: Universal needles #70/10 for sheers;
  #80/12 or #90/14 for heavier fabrics

1 Cut a circle of fabric the
circumference of the tabletop
adding ½" to the edge for the seam
allowance.

2 Cut one rectangle of fabric
twice the circumference of
the tabletop plus 1" by the
height of the table from the
tabletop to the floor plus 8" for
the hem.

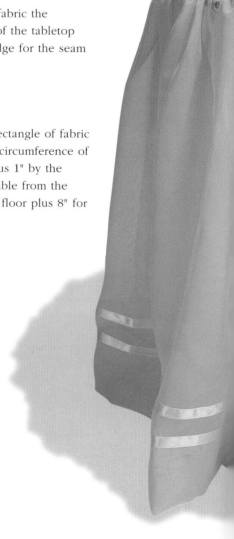

3 Press under 4" along the lower long edge of the rectangle. Press up 4" again for the hem and pin. Using the longest stitch length or your built-in basting stitch, machine-baste the hem in place.

HANDY HINT

On sheer fabrics, it is advisable to use a double-fold hem to avoid any uneven fabric edges from showing through to the right side.

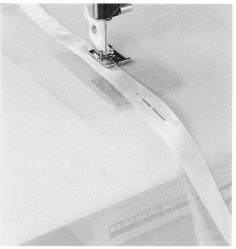

4 Pin the ribbon over the machine basting line at the hem. Edgestitch the ribbon along both long edges using your blindhem or edgestitch foot. Adjust your needle position if necessary.

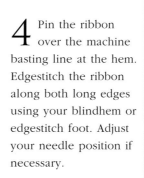

HANDY HINT

Adjust your presser foot pressure if the fabric and ribbon tend to slide under the foot.

continued

6 With right sides together, stitch the short ends of the rectangle together using a ½" seam creating a tube. Trim the seam to ¼" and zigzag along the cut edge to finish the seam.

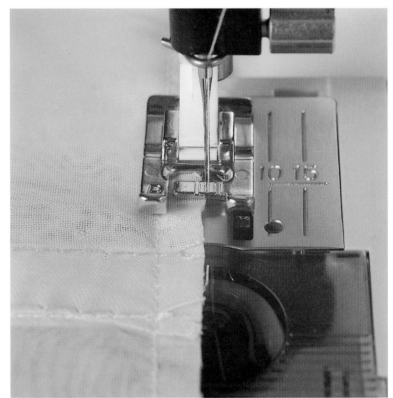

5 Measure 1" up from the stitched ribbon and mark a line with a fabric marking pen. Place a second ribbon over the marking and pin. Stitch both long edges in place. Press the ribbons carefully.

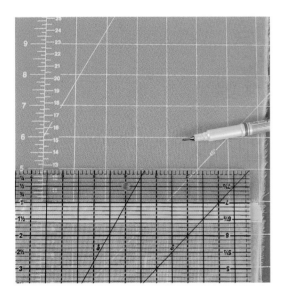

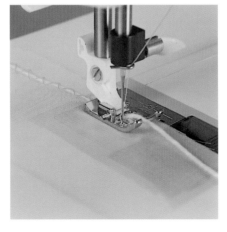

7 To gather the upper edge of the tablecloth, cut a piece of string or gimp cord slightly longer than the circumference of the fabric. Set your machine for a wide and long zigzag stitch. Place the cord under the back of the presser foot (decorative foot) and up over the front of the toes on the foot. Stitch over the cord about ¼" from the edge making sure the cord is within the zigzag stitch.

HANDY HINT

Another method of gathering is to use a gathering foot. Stitch out a sample to test the amount of gathering before stitching your project.

9 With the gathered side on top, stitch the ½" seam being careful not to catch the cord in the stitching. Remove the string.

10 Trim the seam allowance and zigzag the edge to clean-finish. Press.

8 Before gathering the edge, divide the fabric into quarters and mark. Fold the top circle into quarters and mark. With right sides together, pin the circle to the side section at the quarter markings. Pull up on the cord sliding the fabric along the cord to gather and fit.

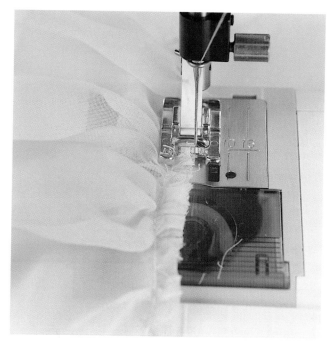

REVERSIBLE PATIO
TABLECLOTH

This reversible round tablecloth can be used indoors

or out. Any length will work from a casual drop to floor length.

VOCABULARY

Drop length—amount of fabric that hangs over the edge of a tabletop.

Finger-press—gently crease fabric with pressure from your fingers.

Notch—to cut small triangles of fabric from the seam allowance on concave curves to allow the seam to lie flat.

TECHNIQUES YOU WILL LEARN

- Determining yardage for a circular tablecloth
- Matching patterns
- Sewing circles
- Notching curves

*Supplies are given for a 48"-diameter table with a 12" drop

Fabric: 4¹/₂ yards each of two coordinating decorator fabrics

Notions: 5 yards of cotton-covered jumbo cording

　Matching sewing thread

　Fabric marking pen

　Tape measure

　Yardstick

Needles: Universal needles #80/12

Other supplies: Pins and string

1 Measure the diameter of the tabletop. Add 12" times two for the drop length plus 1" for each of the seam allowances. This is the length/width of your fabric.

2 It may be necessary to piece your fabric to accommodate the complete diameter measurement from Step 1. Use a full width of fabric for the center panel by your measurement length/width. Cut two side panels wide enough to equal the measurement length/width. Cut the reversible side of fabric the same size as the top piecing as necessary.

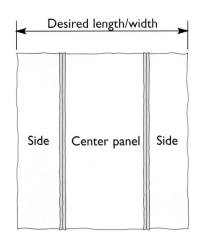

Desired length/width

Side | Center panel | Side

HANDY HINT

To determine the yardage needed for your tablecloth, divide the measurement you calculated in Step 1 by 36". Be sure to allow enough fabric for matching prints.

3 If your fabric has a distinct design pattern, you will need to match the pattern at the seams. From the right side, fold under ½" along the side panel edge and finger-press. Lay the folded edge over the center panel of fabric and match the pattern. Pin in place from the top.

continued

4 Using a long zigzag stitch and a loosened top tension, stitch along the fold so the swing of the zigzag stitch just pierces the fold.

5 Turn the fabric to the wrong side and open out the fold. You will see a ladder-type stitch has been formed. Stitch the panels, right sides together, with a straight stitch using the ladder stitches as a guide. Open the seam and press.

HANDY HINT

For fabrics that do not require matching, join the center fabric panel to each side panel, right sides together, using $1/2$" seams forming a square of fabric.

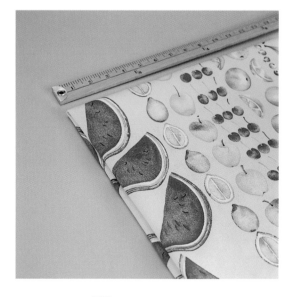

6 Fold the pieced square into quarters and pin the layers together. Using a yardstick measure down from the center folded corner the radius of the cloth (e.g. for a table 18" in diameter, measure 9").

7 Tie the string to a pin attaching the other end to the fabric-marking pen. The length of the string is equal to the radius of the finished cloth plus ½" (e.g. 9" plus ½"). With the pin at the center, pivot and draw a line from one edge of the folded fabric to the other. Cut on the marked line. Repeat the same procedure on the reversible side fabric.

HANDY HINT

The zipper foot is the best foot to use when applying jumbo cord. By moving the needle position, you can stitch very close to the cord.

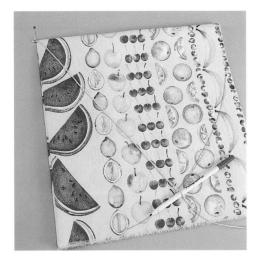

8 Pin the covered cording to the edge of the circle and baste in place using a zipper foot to the right of the needle. Clip the seam allowance and the cording lip to ease around the curves.

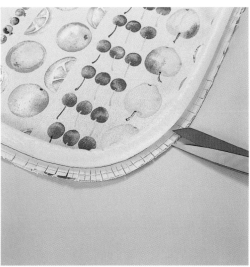

9 With right sides together, stitch the two layers of tablecloth using a zipper foot moving the needle close to crowd the cording. Leave a 12" opening for turning. Notch the curves before turning.

10 Turn the cloth right side out by pulling the tablecloth fabric through the opening. Press. Slipstitch the opening closed.

BASKET
LINERS &
ORGANIZERS

WICKER
BASKET LINERS

*These simple basket liners are ideal as a beginning sewing
project. Coordinate the lining fabric with your room decor
for added pizzazz.*

VOCABULARY

Casing with header—stitched channel with extra
fabric above; serves as a ruffle when gathered on a
rod or with a ribbon; used on café curtains, on
valances, and along casings where added fabric
interest is needed.

TECHNIQUES
YOU WILL LEARN

- Making a pattern
- Making a casing with header
- Making ties

Fabric: Fabric of choice — yardage based on size of
  basket
Notions: Matching sewing thread
  Grided pattern tracing paper
  Fabric marking pen
  Pencil
  Tape measure
Needles: Universal needles #80/12
Other supplies: Decorative basket(s)
  Large safety pin (bodkin optional)

1 Trace the bottom of the
basket on pattern tracing
paper. Add a ½" seam
allowance to all sides. Cut one
fabric piece for the bottom.

2 Using a flexible tape measure, measure the upper edge of the basket from the center of one side to the center of the opposite side and add 1" for seam allowances.

3 Measure the depth of the basket and add 4½" for the seam allowance, casing, and header. Using the measurements from Steps 2 and 3, cut two fabric rectangles for the sides.

HANDY HINT

The ruffle can be omitted from this project if desired. Allow only 2½" for the seam allowance and the casing.

continued

4 Pin the short sides, right sides together, and place a mark 8" from the top edge on both sides for the opening for the handles. Baste the basket sides using your longest stitch length and making ½" seams; stop stitching at the mark and backstitch.

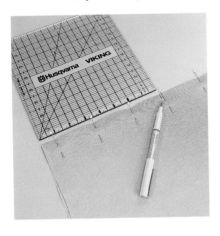

5 Without removing the fabric from under the presser foot, change the stitch length to a standard straight stitch (2.5 mm or 10-12 stitches per inch). Finish stitching to the end of the fabric.

6 Press the seams open. Press under ¼" along the edges of the seam allowance and pin. Edgestitch to clean-finish the seams using your blindhem or edgestitching foot. Remove the basting stitches from the mark to the top edge.

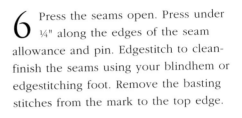

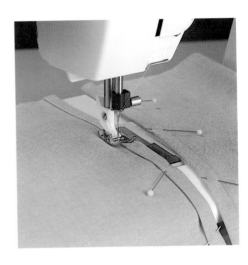

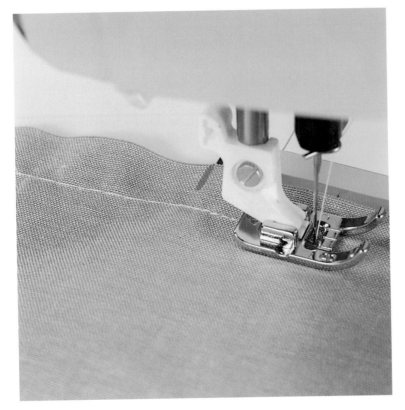

7 To form the casing and ruffle, press under ½" along the long upper edge of the liner. Press under again 3½". Edgestitch close to the pressed edge.

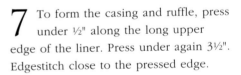

8 Draw a line 1½" from the top edge and stitch along the line forming the header.

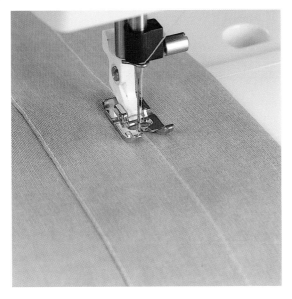

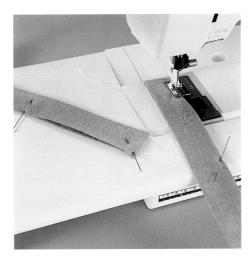

10 Cut two ties 3" wide by the measurement from Step 2 plus 24" for the bows. Press under ½" along all the edges. Fold the ties in half lengthwise, wrong sides together, and press. Edgestitch close to the pressed edges.

9 With right sides together, pin the bottom section to the side section. If your basket is wider at the top and narrower at the bottom, you will need to pleat in some of the fabric to fit the bottom. To do this at the seam, fold in equal amounts of fabric on each side of the seam at both ends. Stitch the bottom to the side section using ½" seam allowance.

11 Attach a safety pin to the end of each tie and thread through the casings at the top edge. Insert the liner into the basket and tighten the ties to pull up any fullness in the liner. Tie the ends into a bow.

LAUNDRY
HAMPER LINERS

Add a little color to your laundry woes! These fun hamper liners can easily be removed and carried to the washing machine. Coordinate a wastebasket liner, too.

VOCABULARY

Welt seam—type of seam with one seam allowance trimmed, both allowances pressed to one side and topstitched.

TECHNIQUES YOU WILL LEARN

- Making a pattern
- Making easy ties
- Stitching a welt seam

---

*Fabric quantities are given for one 18"-tall hamper.

Fabric: 1 yard of 44"/45"-wide fabric for laundry bag

  ½ yard of 44"/45"-wide contrasting fabric for flap and ties

Notions: Grided pattern tracing paper

  Fabric marking pen

  Seam gauge

  Matching sewing thread

Needles: Universal needles #80/12

Other supplies: Galvanized can, bucket, or wicker baskets

  Notepad and pencil

  Safety pin (bodkin optional)

1 Place your can or hamper on grided pattern tracing paper. Using a pencil, trace around the bottom of the can. Using a seam gauge, add a ½" seam allowance outside the circumference of the tracing. Cut along the outside marking with scissors. Cut one circle from your fabric.

HANDY HINT

Keep your good sewing shears reserved for cutting fabric only. Cutting paper will dull the edges.

2 Measure the height of the can; add 1" for seam allowances and jot down the measurement. Measure the circumference at the upper edge of the can; add 1" for the seam allowance and jot down. Measure the circumference of the bottom pattern piece and jot down the measurement. Cut a pattern for the bag using these measurements. The top will be slightly wider than the bottom. Cut one piece from the fabric.

3 With right sides together, fold the bag in half matching the raw edges. Stitch using a ½" seam allowance to form a tube.

continued

4 To clean-finish the seam, trim
one side of the seam allowance
to ¼" wide. Press the seam allowances
to one side with the trimmed side
underneath making a flatter seam.
Turn the tube right side out.

6 To construct the bottom, begin
by press-marking the fabric
circle. Fold the circle in half and then
in quarters and press along the folds.
Next, divide the tube into quarters
and mark with a fabric marker.

5 Make a welt seam by guiding the
foot along the seamline and
stitching down the seam allowance
underneath.

HANDY HINT

Use an Edge/Joining foot
with a flange, for making
welt seams. The flange
rides in the seam for
accurate, straight
stitching.

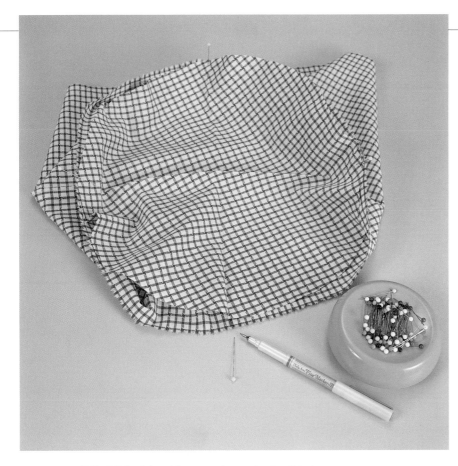

7 With right sides together, pin the fabric circle to the tube matching your pess markings to the quarter markings first. Continue pinning around the circle keeping the cut edges even. Stitch using a ½" seam allowance. Clean-finish the seam allowance with a zigzag stitch or a serger.

8 Cut four flap strips from the contrasting fabric, 4½" wide by half the circumference of the upper edge of the can plus 1". With right sides together, stitch two strips together along one lengthwise edge. Repeat for the remaining strips.

9 Press the seams open. Press under ½" along each short end on both strips. Topstitch the short ends down using a left needle position.

continued

10 Turn the flaps to the right side and press flat. Edgestitch along the finished long edge moving your needle as far right as possible.

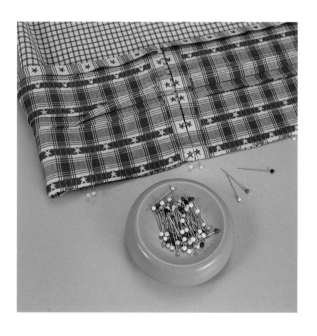

11 Beginning at the bag side seam, pin the right side of the flap to the wrong side of bag. Pin the remaining flap to the bag butting the ends together. Stitch with a ½" seam allowance.

12 Press under ½" along the remaining long edge of the flap. Pin the pressed edge over the seam allowance and edgestitch close to the pressed edge.

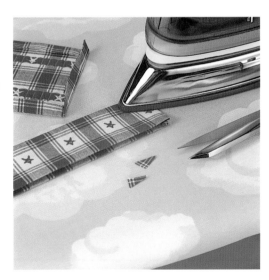

13 Measure the width of one flap and draw a line through the middle. Stitch following the line to form a casing for the ties.

14 Cut two strips of fabric for ties 4" wide by half the top circumference of the can plus 24" for tying. Press under ¼" along all cut edges of ties. Fold the ties in half lengthwise, trim corners, and press.

15 Edgestitch, using your blindhem or edgestitching foot, around the three pressed sides of the ties. Thread the ties through the casings on the flaps.

HANDY HINT

Attach a safety pin to the end of each tie to help guide it through the casing. A bodkin can also be used instead of the safety pin.

Stair Basket
GARTER

Ribbon and fabric are the perfect embellishment for this handy stair basket. Try the clever sewing trick to make this beautiful ribbon rose.

VOCABULARY

Bartack—very narrow, dense line of zigzag stitching used to hold layers in place.

TECHNIQUES YOU WILL LEARN

• Making a bartack bow
• Making an elastic casing

Fabric: ¹/₂ yard of decorator fabric
Notions: ¹/₂"-wide elastic — yardage equal to circumference of basket plus 1"
  1 yard of 1¹/₂"-wide ribbon
  1 yard of ³/₈"-wide ribbon
  Matching sewing thread
  Hand-sewing needle
  Fabric marking pen
  Ruler or tape measure
Needles: Universal needles #80/12
Other supplies: Tube turner (optional)
  Safety pin (elastic guide or bodkin, optional)

1 Measure the circumference of the basket. Multiply the circumference by two and add 1" for the cut length. The cut width is 7". Example: The circumference of our basket is 43". To make the garter, a strip 87" long by 7" wide was needed. Cut the elastic the entire circumference of the basket plus 1".

HANDY HINT

Cut two 7"-wide strips of fabric the entire width of the fabric and seam together, then cut the new strip down to make a strip 87" long.

2 Fold the long edges of the strip of fabric, right sides together, and pin. Sew along the edge with a ½" seam allowance. Turn the fabric tube right side out and press with the seam in the center.

3 Measuring from the needle out to the right side, apply a piece of masking tape to the arm of your sewing machine to mark a 1⅛" seam allowance. Guide the finished edge of the fabric along the edge of the tape to sew one side of the casing. Turn the fabric and sew the other side of the casing again guiding the edge of the fabric along the tape.

continued

4 Insert the elastic in the center casing with a safety pin. Carefully draw the length of the elastic into the fabric casing until the end of the elastic is even with the edge of the fabric. Pin through the fabric and elastic to prevent the elastic from being pulled through. Pull the elastic out of the casing at the other end and pin with edges even.

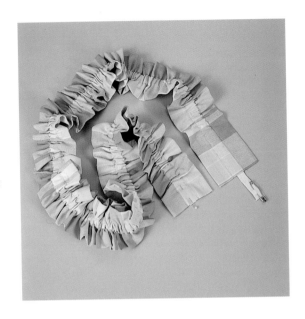

HANDY HINT

An elastic guide or bodkin are useful tools to own for threading elastics, ribbons, or ties through casings.

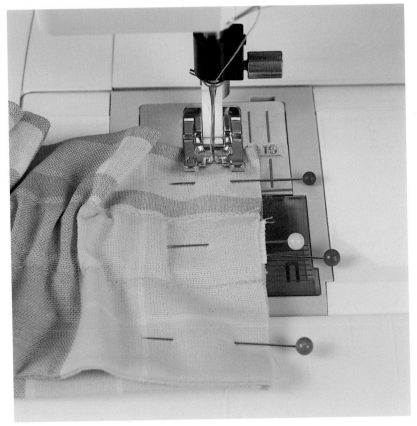

5 Place the short ends of the fabric band right sides together. Pin and sew the seam to secure the elastic. Press the seam open.

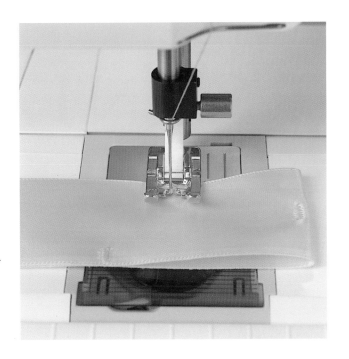

6 To make the bow, fold the ribbons in half with the narrower ribbon centered inside. Stitch the ribbons together with a bartack of stitching ¼" long and ¼" away from the fold with a narrow zigzag with a short stitch length, or use a bartack stitch on your machine.

7 Place marks along one of the long edges of the ribbon beginning at the folded edge at 1½", 5", 7½", 12" and 15". Along the other edge of the ribbon, mark 2¼", 4½", 8¼", 11¼" and 16" from the fold. Using the same narrow zigzag or bartack stitch, sew tacks on both sides of the ribbon at the marks being careful not to catch the inner ribbon in the stitching.

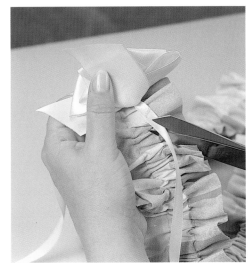

HANDY HINT

Check your sewing machine manual to see if you have a bartack or a pre-programmed satin stitch. Narrow the width to about 1.5mm for this technique.

8 Hold onto the inner ribbon and slide the wide ribbon into a bow. Place the bow over the seam of the garter. Spread the tails of the inner ribbon underneath the tails of the wide ribbon bow and pin. Flip the wide bow away and tack the inner ribbon to the garter with a few hand stitches. Trim away the excess ribbon. Use this ribbon bow on presents, too!

Bath Towel
ORGANIZER

For extra storage space in a small bath or powder room, make this handy

bath towel organizer for on a wall or the back of the door.

VOCABULARY

Backstitch—to take a few stitches backward at the beginning and end of a seam to prevent the seam from raveling out.

Casing—a stitched channel used on simple curtains or valances to hold the curtain rod. Casings are also used for waistbands or on sleeves to hold elastic bands.

TECHNIQUES
YOU WILL LEARN

- Making casings
- Backstitching
- Stitching through thicknesses

Fabric: Set of three coordinating cotton dish towels (size: 18" by 27")

Notions: 2¹/₂ yards of ¹/₂" cotton cording

Matching sewing thread

Ruler or tape measure

Fabric marking pen

Needles: Universal needles #80/12

Other supplies: Three 24"-long dowel rods, ⁵/₈" in diameter

Six 1¹/₂" head beads with 0.59" opening

Wood glue

1 Set the towel with the decorative band aside to be used for the top pocket of the organizer. Bring the short ends of one towel together with the wrong side folded inside. This will be the bottom pocket.

2 Lay a second towel out flat with the wrong side down. Place the folded towel on top of the flat towel with the short ends 8" down from the top short end of the flat towel.

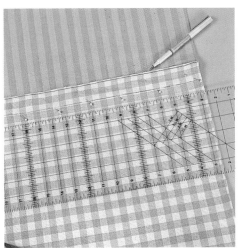

3 Pin through all three layers along the short
hemmed ends. Use a fabric marking pen to
draw a stitching line along the hemmed edge of the
folded towel. Draw another line 1¼" below the first
line. Sew with a straight stitch following both lines
making a casing. Backstitch at the beginning and
end of each line to reinforce your seam.

continued

4 Bring the short ends of the flat towel together to make the middle pocket.

5 Take the remaining towel and fold the decorative band plus 1½" toward the wrong side of the towel. Use an iron to press a crease.

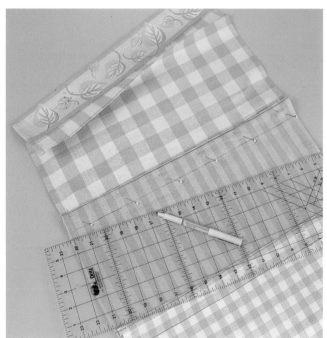

6 Lay the towel with the decorative band out flat with the wrong side down. Place the lower and middle pocket, right side down, on the flat towel with the short ends of the middle pocket 8" down from the crease on the flat towel like you did in Step 2.

7 Pin, mark, and sew a casing as you did in Step 3.

8 Bring the short end of the flat towel to the crease. Then, fold the decorative band toward the front of the pocket at the crease line. Use a fabric marking pen to draw a line near the folded edge of the top pocket. Draw another line 1¼" below the first line. Sew on the lines. Insert a dowel rod in each casing.

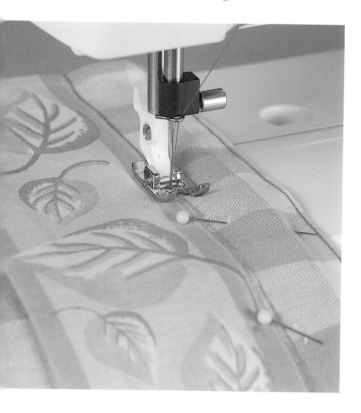

9 Beginning on one side of the organizer at the lower dowel rod, tie a knot in the cord leaving a 5" tail. Connect the cord to each rod and knot. At the top of the organizer, leave 22" slack for hanging. Once the cording is knotted at each rod, untwist the cord tails below the lower rod to make tassels. Trim the threads of the tassels even. A touch of glue at each knot will keep the knots from shifting.

HANDY HINT

If the threads of your tassel cording retain the "curl" from being twisted, then lightly spray the threads with starch. Comb the threads to smooth them for a "tamer" tassel.

10 Glue a head bead on the end of each dowel rod.

ORGANIZER
FOR BABY'S ROOM

*Hang this handy organizer from the changing table or on
the end of the baby's crib. Made from a bath towel, ribbon,
and fabric, this is a great gift for any new mother.*

TECHNIQUES YOU WILL LEARN

- Making narrow hems
- Basting
- Adding decorative trim
- Sewing terry cloth fabric
- Adjusting needle positions

Fabric: ⁷/₈ yard of coordinating fabric
Notions: ²/₃ yard of ⁵/₈"-wide grosgrain ribbon
   Matching sewing thread
   Fabric marking pen
   Ruler or tape measure
Needles: Universal needles #80/12
Other supplies: Bath towel

1 Cut two rectangles from the fabric 22" by 24" for the over-pocket. Cut one fabric band the length and width of the woven band on the towel plus ½".

2 Baste along all four sides of the fabric band with a ¼" seam allowance. Using the stitching line as your guide, press the seam allowances to the wrong side.

HANDY HINT

When stitching heavier fabrics, lengthen your stitch slightly to about 3.0 - 3.5 mm.

3 Lay the fabric band, wrong side down, over the woven band on the towel. Pin the band in place and topstitch close to the folded edge along all four sides.

HANDY HINT

Use your blindhem or edgestitching foot to help guide your topstitching on ribbon and fabric trim. Move your needle position so the stitching is close to the edge.

continued

4 Fold up a 10" pocket along the end of the towel with the topstitched band so the band is on the outside. Pin the side edges together. Sew the side seams to hold the pocket in place. Divide the width of the pocket into thirds and draw two stitching lines with a fabric marking pen. Sew over the lines.

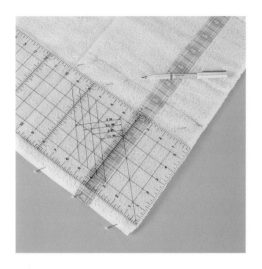

5 Cut the length of the towel to 31".

6 Lay one over-pocket piece out flat with the right side up. Pin the grosgrain ribbon along one 22" side 1¼" away from the cut edge of the fabric. Topstitch along both edges of the ribbon.

7 Place the two over-pocket pieces right sides together. Pin three edges together leaving open the side opposite the one trimmed with ribbon. Sew along the pinned edges removing the pins as you sew. Trim the seam allowances at both corners. Turn the over-pocket right side out and press.

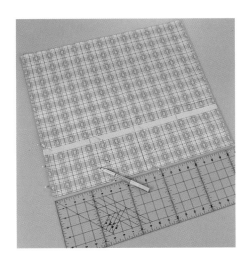

8 Fold the ribbon-trimmed edge up 6" and pin. Sew the side seams. Divide the width of the over-pocket into fourths and draw three stitching lines. Sew over the lines.

9 Lay the towel out flat with the right side up. Center the over-pocket on top of the towel pinning the cut edges of the over-pocket and towel together. Fold a 2½" casing to the back of the towel and pin. Draw a stitching line 2" from the folded edge. Flip the over-pocket away from the towel as shown. Sew over the line. Reinforce the seam with a 3-step zigzag along the cut edges of the casing.

HANDY HINT

The 3-step zigzag is used to prevent the loosely woven terry cloth from raveling away from a straight stitch.

SILVERWARE
CADDY

*Make your picnics more fun with these practical but creative silverware
caddies. Hang them on the back of the chair or roll them up for carrying to the get-together.*

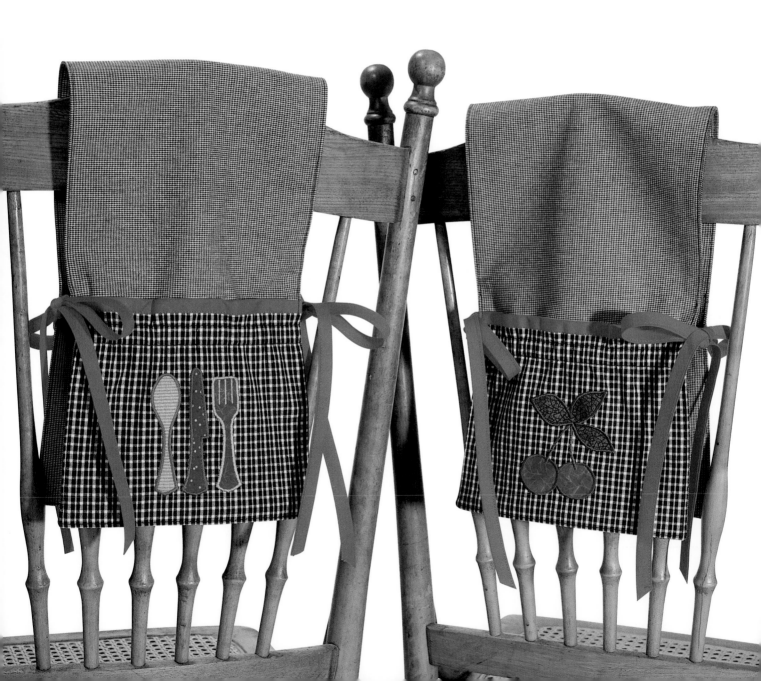

1 From the 1/2 yard of fabric, cut two 9" by 29" rectangles for the caddy. Cut a 9" square pocket from the contrasting fabric. Cut four 18" lengths of the double-fold bias tape for ties and one 9" length for pocket trim. Cut an 8" length of elastic.

2 Along one edge of the pocket piece, press 2" to the wrong side of the fabric.

continued

DESIGN  OPTIONS

Embellish the pocket piece with appliqué, embroidery, ribbons, or buttons before stitching it to the caddy fabric. Follow the manufacturer's instructions on the paper-backed fusible web for appliqué techniques. Satin-stitch around the raw edges. Or use one of today's computerized sewing and embroidery machines which offer unlimited decorative options including automatic appliqué or embroidery designs.

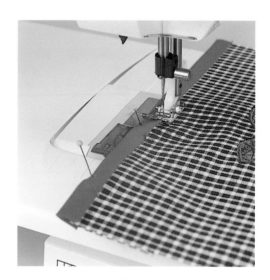

3 To find the center of the pocket for decorative embellishments, fold the pocket piece in half and make a crease. Using a seam gauge, mark the center on crease line 3¼" from the raw edge. Add appliqués or embroideries at this time to the flat fabric.

4 Enclose the folded edge of the pocket inside the fold of the bias tape. Place the narrower side of the tape on the right side of pocket. Edgestitch along the edge of the bias tape sewing both sides at the same time.

5 Sew an elastic casing inside the bias tape trimmed-edge of the pocket. Sew the first line of stitching positioning the right edge of the standard presser foot next to the edge of the bias tape or ⅜" away. Draw a second stitching line ¾" from the first line of stitching. Sew following the line.

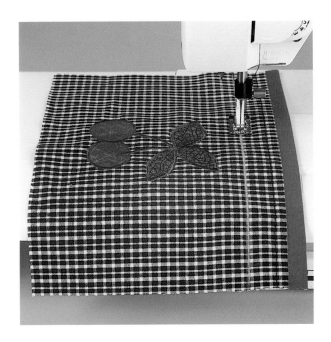

HANDY HINT

On double-fold bias tape, notice that one side is slightly wider than the other side. When stitching the tape down, stitch the tape down from the narrower side. Your stitches will catch the wider edge underneath at the same time.

6 Draw the elastic piece into the casing. Pin the ends of the elastic even with edges of pocket.

continued

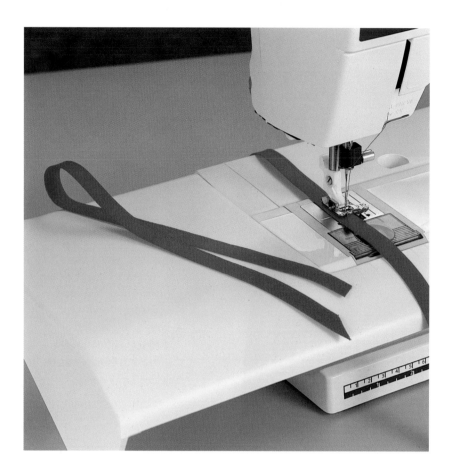

8 Lay a caddy piece out flat, right side up, and pin the pocket, right side up, along a short edge. Pin the ties on both sides of the pocket even with the pocket trim. Pin the remaining ties, 7" from the short end opposite the pocket. Make sure the ties are pinned in the same place by folding the short sides of the caddy piece together.

7 To finish each tie, edgestitch the edges closed.

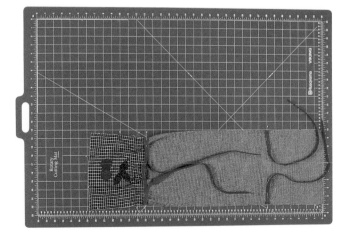

9 Pin the second caddy piece, right sides together, with the one prepared in Step 8. Make sure the ties are inside of the fabric edges. Sew around the rectangle leaving a 3" opening at the short end opposite the pocket. Trim the corners and turn right side out. Press.

10 Edgestitch around the outside of the caddy using your blindhem or edgestitching foot and adjustable needle positions.

11 Stretch the elastic across the pocket so it lies flat in the center of the pocket. Sew through the elastic and fabric layer to tack the center of the pocket to the caddy. Reinforce the stitching by backstitching.

TAB TOPS, WINDOW TOPPERS, & CURTAINS

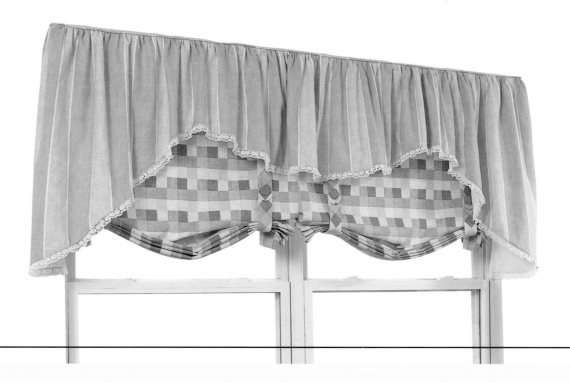

Tabbed-Bottom
PULL SHADE

These easy-to-make fabric-covered roller shades may be just

the answer for privacy and decoration in the kitchen.

VOCABULARY

Air-soluble—marks that disappear after time in the air.

Water-soluble—marks that disappear with water application.

Seam sealant—notion that secures seams, threads, and prevents fraying on edges.

Sunbrella® fabric—brand of fabric that will not fade or deteriorate from the sun; mildew resistent.

TECHNIQUES YOU WILL LEARN

• Measuring a window

Fabric: Decorator fabric the finished length plus 12" for rolling

Notions: Commercial shade kit, such as Pellon® Wonder Shade or pull shade, slat for bottom and mounting hardware

    Seam sealant spray

    Air-soluble marking pen

    Matching sewing thread

    Tape measure and ruler

Needles: Universal needles #80/12

Other supplies: Wood or metal decorative rod for bottom of shade the length equal to width of finished shade

1 Install the mounting hardware for the shade in the window before cutting your fabric. Make sure the roller sits in the hardware exactly as it will when the shade is completed. Adjust the width of the roller shade according to the manufacturer's instructions to fit.

2 If you are covering a premade roller shade, measure the window for either an inside or outside mounted shade. For an inside mount, it is best to install the hardware before measuring your window.

3 Cut the decorator fabric the width of the finished shade plus an additional inch at each side by the length of the finished shade plus 12". Cut four 4" by 7" strips for the tabs.

continued

4 Follow the instructions on the shade kit to complete or complete the shade as follows: Using an air-soluble marking pen, mark the exact width of the finished shade on the fabric. Set your sewing machine to the "lightning" or straight stretch stitch and sew along the line on each side.

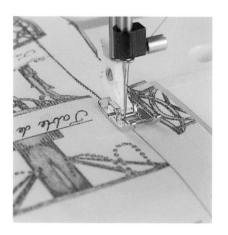

HANDY HINT

The shade kit we selected came with room-darkening fusible fabric that should be fused to the decorator fabric. During a test-fuse required in the kit instructions, we realized that our Sunbrella® fabric shrinks quite a bit in the fusing process. We chose not to use the room-darkening fabric.

HANDY HINT

Hold the fabric taut in the front and back while stitching to ensure the fabric lies perfectly flat when complete.

5 On the wrong side of the fabric, spray seam sealant along the stitched lines following the manufacturer's instructions. When the sealant is dry, trim very close to the stitching.

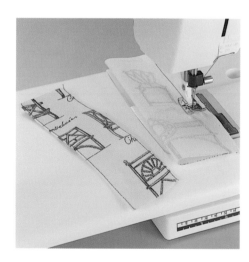

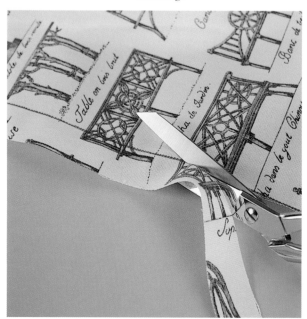

6 Make the tabs by folding right sides together along the long edge. Stitch and turn. Position the seam in the center back of the tab and edgestitch close to the fold on each side.

7 On the wrong side of the fabric, mark a line 3" up from the bottom of the shade. Fold the tabs in half with the seam to the inside. Measure the finished width of the shade. Pin the four tabs equally spaced along the bottom of the shade so the raw edges of the tabs are ½" beyond the marked line and the folded edge of the tabs face toward the top of the shade. Check the length of the tabs with a seam gauge to make sure they are exactly even. Stitch along the marked line.

9 Fold the tabs toward the bottom of the shade. Check the length again with a seam gauge. Pin. Edgestitch along the lower edge of the casing, catching the tabs in the stitching. Insert the slat in the casing.

8 At the bottom of the shade, fold ½" to the wrong side. Pin the folded edge just above the stitched line created in Step 7 to form the casing for the slat. Stitch again on the previous stitching line.

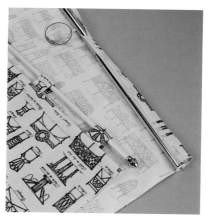

10 Using masking tape or a staple gun, adhere the shade to the roller across the top edge. Roll up the shade by hand evenly. Turn the flat mechanism at one end of the roller shade to wind the shade. Insert the finished shade into the mounting hardware and place a decorative rod in the tabs.

TAB-TOPPED BED FRAME
ORGANIZER

*Your child will love this handy bed frame organizer for his
or her favorite T-shirts, socks, or magazines.*

VOCABULARY

Gusset—piece of fabric inserted at sides for wider opening.

TECHNIQUES YOU WILL LEARN

• Making gusset pockets
• Stitch-in-the-ditch
• Adding Velcro® brand tape

Fabric: 2 yards of canvas
    1 yard of two different cotton plaids
Notions: 6" of 1"-wide Velcro® brand Soft &
    Flexible SEW-ON tape
    48" of double-fold bias tape
    Matching sewing thread
    Ruler, seam gauge, or tape measure
    Fabric marking pen
Needles: Universal or Jeans needles #80/12 or
    #90/14 depending on the weight of the canvas

1 Cut one rectangle, 32" by 24", from the canvas for the base panel. Cut six rectangles, 3" by 12", for the tabs. Cut two rectangles of each plaid, 12" by 15½", for the pockets.

2 Zigzag all the edges of the canvas panel to prevent raveling.

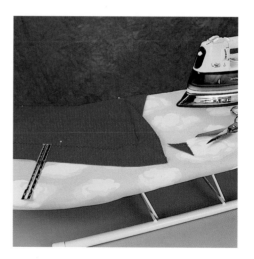

3 Fold under 2" hems on all four sides of the canvas panel. Trim the corners to reduce bulk. Stitch the hems close to the edges on all sides.

HANDY HINT

For another method of applying bias trim, use fusible thread on your bobbin. After stitching along the fold, wrap the tape around the edge and press. The tape will be fused in place for the next line of stitching.

4 Cut the bias tape into four 12" lengths. Open out half of the bias tape and pin each piece, matching the raw edges, to the 12" edge of each pocket. Stitch to the upper edge of the pocket using the fold line as your stitching line.

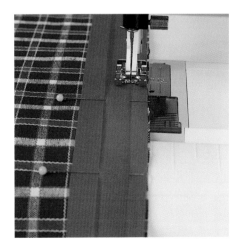

continued

5 Wrap the tape around the edge and press in place. Pin and "stitch-in-the-ditch" using your edgestitch or blindhem foot and moving the needle position close to the edge.

6 Using a 3-step zigzag stitch, edgestitch on the remaining three sides of each pocket.

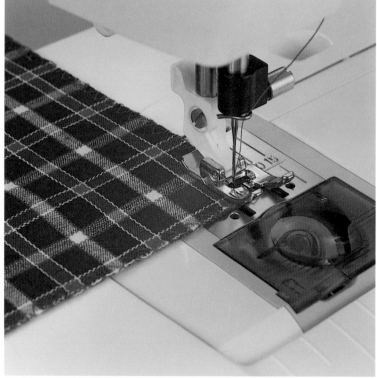

7 Fold under ½" hems on all three sides of the pockets. On the right side, measure in 1" at both long side edges of each pocket. Press. Fold the side edges back on themselves forming a gusset.

HANDY HINT

Fold the fabric at a diagonal at the corners first before folding in the sides to reduce bulk and give a clean finish.

8 From the right side, edgestitch along the folded edge for the gusset to hold it in place. Baste along the bottom edge of each pocket piece to hold the pleat in place.

continued

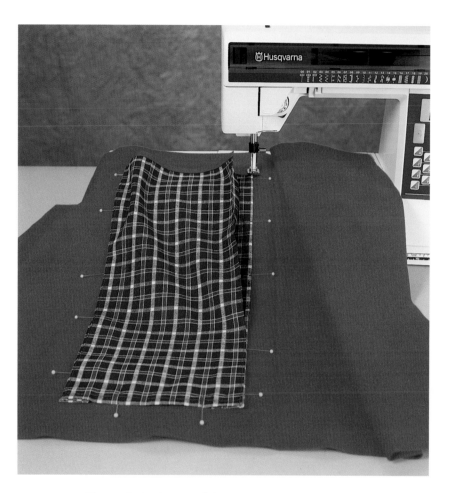

10 Pin and stitch the other center pocket, butting the edges on the center mark. Repeat the stitching for the other pockets, alternating the plaids.

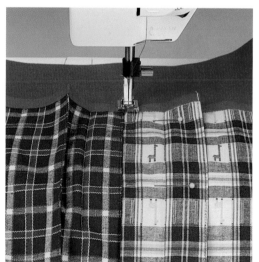

9 Mark the center of the canvas panel. Measure up 2" from the lower edge and pin one pocket in place. Stitch close to the edges using your edgestitch or blindhem foot.

11 To make tabs, press under ½" on the upper edge of each tab piece. Fold the tab in thirds overlapping the edges slightly. Using a flatlock stitch on your machine, stitch the overlapped seam down the center.

12 Stitch the loop side of a 1" Velcro® brand Soft & Flexible SEW-ON square to the finished edge of each tab. Sew around all four edges using your blindhem or edgestitch foot and a longer stitch length. Fold under ½" on the other end of the tab.

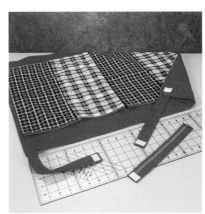

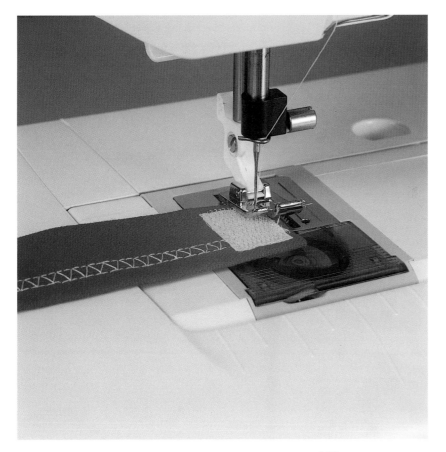

13 Pin the tabs at each end of the panel and equidistant from each other across the center; stitch in place. Add the other side of the Velcro® brand square to the back of the organizer.

REVERSIBLE CAFÉ CURTAIN AND APRON
VALANCE

Rickrack and geometrically shaped pockets add spice to these fun café curtains.

Add a coordinating valance to complete the window treatment.

VOCABULARY

Café Curtain—used most often on double-hung windows, a short curtain the length of which is slightly greater than the window split.

Return—section of cutain or valance from one corner of rod to wall.

Valance—a topper for full length curtains or drapes, or used to visually connect short curtains that only cover part of the window; usually 10"-16" in length.

TECHNIQUES YOU WILL LEARN

- Attaching rick rack
- Simple appliqué
- Measuring a valance

Fabric: Decorator fabric or calicos and coordinating lining — yardage determined by window size (four panels will be cut for the café curtain)

Notions: Buttons
  Matching and coordinating narrow and wide rickrack trims
  Fusible web for appliqués
  Chalk marker
  Air-soluble marking pen
  Grided pattern tracing paper
  Matching sewing thread

Needles: Universal needles #80/12

Other supplies: 2" standard rod for valance
  Tension rod to fit window for café curtain
  Craft paper
  Paper scissors
  Permanent marking pen
  Seam sealant
  Tear-away stabilizer

1 For the valance, mount the standard rod hardware 2"-3" outside of the window casing on each side.

2 To determine the valance fabric cut-width, measure between the hardware, multiply by one and one half for fullness, add 5" for the returns, and 1" for seam allowances. For example, for a finished valance 38" wide, multiply 38" x 1.5 = 57"; 57" + 5" plus 1" = 64" finished cut-width.

4 With right sides together, fold the fabric in half along the long edge and stitch the valance side edges with a ½" seam allowance. Trim the seam and corners, turn, and press. Baste the edges together at the top.

5 Cut the valance apron fabric the width arrived at in Step 2 by 20" long. Cut a lining piece the same measurement. With right sides together, pin and baste the fabric to the lining along the sides and lower edges using a ½" seam allowance.

3 Cut the background fabric for the valance the width determined in Step 2 by two times the desired length, piecing the fabric as necessary to achieve the width.

continued

6 To make a pattern for the apron's scalloped edge, divide the total width of the valance from Step 2 by an odd number of scallops. For example, 64" divided by 5 scallops = 12¾" inches. Cut a piece of craft paper 12¾" wide by 10" high and fold in half along the long edge. Measure up 5" along the open edges. Draw a curved line from the folded edge to the mark on the other edge. With paper scissors, cut along the curved line.

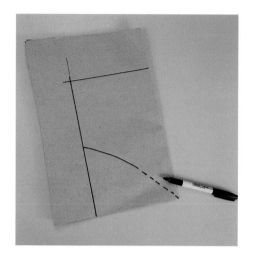

8 Straight-stitch along the basting lines at the sides and along the marked scallop lines at the lower edge of the valance. Trim, clip the curves, and turn the apron to the right side; press. Baste the edges together at the top.

7 Place the folded scallop pattern at the basting line along one side and match the point of the paper pattern to the basting line at the lower edge. Outline the scallop pattern with a chalk marker. Open the pattern and continue marking scallops across the lower edge. End with a half scallop at the opposite edge. The scallops at each side are one half the scallop width. Pin along the chalk line.

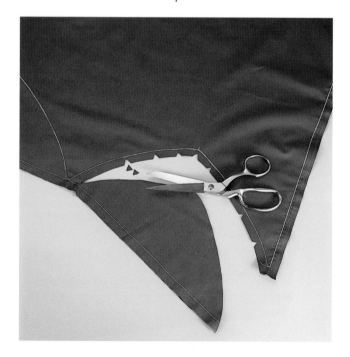

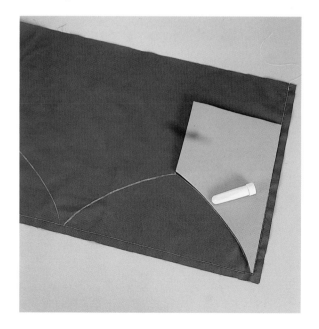

9 Pin wide rickrack to the wrong side of the valance apron so the points of rickrack show behind the scallops. Fold back the cut ends of the rickrack to the wrong side. Topstitch in place. Place a dot of seam sealant on the raw edges of rickrack.

10 With an air-soluble pen, mark a line ¾" from the finished edge of the scallops. Pin a coordinating rickrack trim to the line tucking under ¼" at the cut ends. Topstitch in place.

11 Machine-stitch a decorative button in the center of each scallop point.

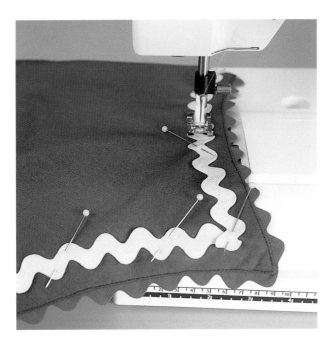

HANDY HINT

Many machines have a built-in stitch for button sewing. If you do not have this stitch on your machine, move the needle position to far left; adjust your stitch width to approximately 3mm. Be sure to turn the handwheel by hand to check the stitch width. Lower the feed teeth to keep the button from moving and stitch. Move the stitch width to 0 to lock the stitching.

continued

12 Pin the valance apron to the background fabric so the scallop points are 1½" above the folded edge. The valance apron will extend 5" above the background fabric. Baste the apron to the background along the top edge. Press down ½" to the lining side of the apron. Press again so the fold meets the basting line where the background is joined to the apron. Edgestitch in place using your blindhem or edgestitch foot. With an air-soluble marking pen, mark a line 2½" from the top folded edge and stitch again to form a header and casing for the curtain rod.

13 Measure the finished length for the café curtain. Add 7" to this measurement for ½" seam allowance and 3" hem at top and bottom of the panels. Add an additional 1" to the length of the fabric panel you will use as the reversible side so the contrasting fabric will show underneath.

HANDY HINT

Make the café curtains slightly longer than one half the window length to cover any hardware in the middle of double-hung windows. The curtains can hang beyond the windowsill or just to the windowsill according to your preference.

14 Determine the finished width of the panels keeping in mind that the tension rod is placed inside the window casing and does not extend beyond the window frame. Add 4" to this measurement for the hems at the side edges of the panels. You will make two panels from each fabric according to this measurement.

15 With an air-soluble marking pen, draw two lines 3½" and 4½" up from the lower edges on the two top panels. Pin contrasting wide rickrack trim along the lines and stitch each row in place.

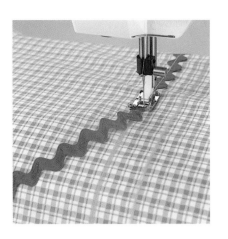

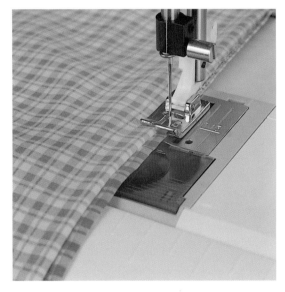

16 Press a 1" double-fold hem on the side edges of all four panels. Pin. Fold the fabric back on itself and, using a blindhem stitch, hem the sides in place.

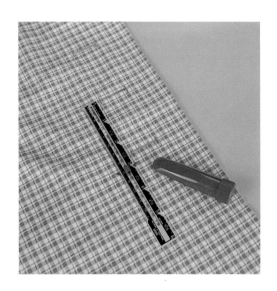

17 Press ½" to the wrong side along the top and bottom edges of each panel, then again 3" more. On the top edge, straight-stitch close to the folded edge to create a facing. Blind-hem the lower edge of each panel folding the fabric as you did in Step 16.

18 For buttonhole placement, measure the finished width and divide by the largest number possible. For example, if the finished panel width is 35"; 35" divided by 8 = 4.37". Fold each panel in half. Starting 2½" down from the top edge measure 2" on each side of the fold and begin marking 1" vertical buttonholes out to each side. Place buttonholes every 4" across the facing. Stitch the same size buttonholes using your buttonhole sensor foot. Cut open.

continued

19 Make a pattern on pattern tracing paper for a 5½" equilateral triangle, a 5" circle, and a 4½" square. Trace the triangle three times on the paper side of the fusible web and trace the circle four times. Press the fusible web to the wrong side of contrasting fabric. Cut out the shapes on the marked lines.

20 Arrange the shapes randomly on the right side of the two top curtain panels, saving space for three shapes that will become pockets. Press in place. With a piece of tear-away stabilizer underneath to stabilize, zigzag over the fused edges to secure.

21 Add a ½" seam allowance to the triangle and square pattern, and cut four squares and two triangles from contrasting fabric for pockets. With right sides together, pin the shapes and stitch around the outside edges using a ½" seam allowance leaving a 2" opening for turning. Trim the seams and clip the corners. Turn and press.

22 Edgestitch coordinating rickrack to all sides of the pockets, tucking under the cut ends to finish. Pin the three pockets on the two top panels with tear-away stabilizer underneath and stitch in place over the previous line of stitching, keeping the top edge open.

23 Pin coordinating rickrack around the remaining fused shapes and topstitch in place, overlapping the cut ends to finish. Remove the stabilizer from the back of the pockets and fused shapes.

24 With the top and bottom café panels layered on top of each other, insert the tension rod through the buttonholes as one.

SHAPED
VALANCE
AND
ROMAN SHADE

These simple window treatments look more complicated to make than they actually are.

Used together or separate, a shaped valance and Roman shade add a nice softness to any window.

VOCABULARY

Roman shade—flat fabric attached to window at the top; fabric is drawn up from the bottom with ring tape.

Shaped valance—valance with curved edge; can be formal or informal depending on the fabric.

TECHNIQUES
YOU WILL LEARN

- Making a shaped valance
- Making a Roman shade

Fabric: Shaped Valance—Decorator fabric three times the length of finished valance (Note: Be sure to allow for matching pattern motif)

Roman shade—Decorator fabric length equal to the window plus 8½"

Lining fabric of equal amount for both

Notions: Gathered Cluny lace two times the width of finished valance

Covered cord with lip the width of window plus 12"

Gimp cord, perle cotton, or dental floss

Two 1½" covered buttons for Roman shade

Lightweight fusible interfacing

Needles: Universal needles #80/12

Other Supplies: Brown craft paper

2" x 4" lumber for valance board

Two L-brackets to attach board to wall

Wood screws

Permanent marking pen

Spring rod(s) for Roman shade

1 Measure 2"-3" on each side and 2"-3" above the window frame for the valance board placement.

2 Install the L-brackets at the marks.

3 Trim the 2" x 4" lumber to fit between the brackets and cover the lumber with muslin or paint the wood to match the window frame. Install with wood screws to the brackets.

continued

4 Determine the finished length of the valance at the sides by measuring to one half the window length; add 1" for seam allowances. For the width, measure from the bracket from side edge to side edge, multiply by two to allow for gathering, and add 1" for seams for the valance width. Piece the decorator fabric to create one panel equal to this width measurement.

HANDY HINT

Decorator fabric comes in widths up to 120". You may need to piece to achieve the width necessary for your window treatment. Remember to match patterns or stripes as directed in earlier projects.

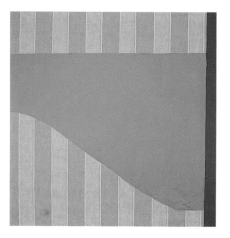

5 To make the pattern for the shaped valance, cut the craft paper the determined valance width and the length from Step 4. Draw a gentle curve on the paper, from side to side, starting 5" in from one side, tapering up then curving gently down for the center section. The center of the valance should be about one half of the finished valance length at the sides. Fold the decorator fabric and pattern paper in half and then place the center edge of the pattern paper on the fold. Cut along the curve. Cut a small notch in the fabric at the center top and bottom. Cut the lining the same.

6 Fold in ¼" twice at the cut end of the lace. Starting ½" from the side edge pin the gathered lace ⅜" from lower edge of the valance, with right sides together. Fold in the opposite end of lace as before. Baste the lace in place.

8 To gather the top edge of the valance, set your zigzag stitch to a 5mm width and 3mm length. Place the end of the gimp cord or perle cotton under the back of the foot leaving a tail and up over the front toes. Zigzag over the perle cotton keeping it free of the stitching. Pull the perle cotton to gather.

7 With right sides together, pin the decorator fabric to the lining. Using a ½" seam allowance, stitch along the sides and lower curved edge. Clip the seams and turn. Baste the top raw edges together.

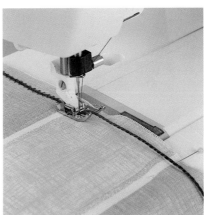

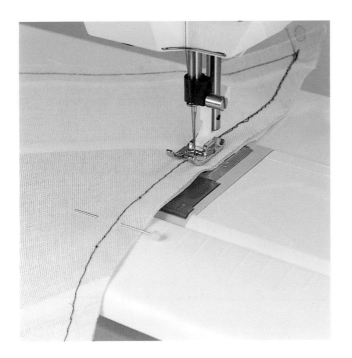

HANDY HINT

Dental floss works very well as a gathering cord under the zigzag stitch. It is very strong and unlikely to break.

continued

9 For the valance band, cut a piece of decorator fabric the same measurement as the covered cornice board plus 1-1/2" by 5" wide. Cut a notch at the center of the front and back. Cut the lining to match. Matching the raw edges, pin the covered cord to the valance band along the sides and front. Fold the excess covered cord toward the raw edge 1/2" from the back edge of the valance band at each side and baste.

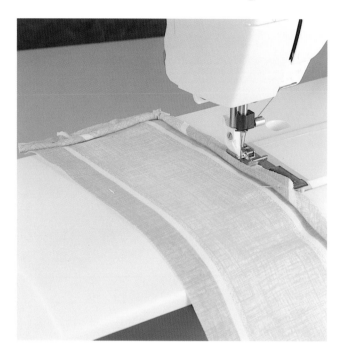

10 With right sides together, pin the shaped valance to the valance band along the sides and front and matching the center notches. Adjust the gathers evenly and stitch.

HANDY HINT

When stitching a gathered piece to a flat piece, place the gathered piece next to the feed teeth. The movement of the teeth against the fabric helps ease the gathers while sewing.

11 Pin the valance band lining to the stitched valance, with right sides together, and stitch along the previous line of stitching at the front and sides. Turn and press.

12 Press ½" seam allowance to the inside on both the decorator fabric and the lining along the open edge of the band. Edgestitch to finish. Use a staple gun or thumb tacks to attach the shaped valance to the top of the board.

14 Treating the lining and decorator fabric as one, press under a 1" double-fold hem along the sides and pin. Select the blindhem foot and the blindhem stitch on your machine. Fold the fabric back on itself like an "S" and stitch just catching the edge.

13 For the Roman shade, cut the fabric and lining equal to the length of the window plus 8½" by the width of the window plus 4". With wrong sides together, pin the fabric to the lining. Baste at the side edges.

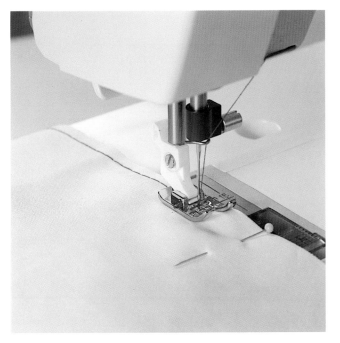

15 Again with the fabric layers as one, press ½" to the wrong side at the top edge. Press down 2" more and pin. Straight-stitch along the pressed edge to form the casing using the blindhem or edgestitch foot.

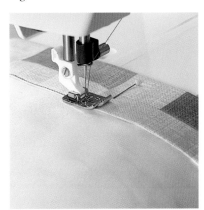

continued

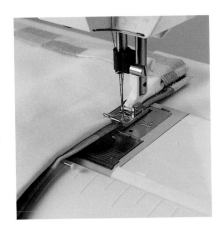

16 Along the bottom edge, press up a 3" double-fold hem. Blind-hem in place as you did on the side hems in Step 14.

17 To make the shade straps, cut two bias strips of fabric 5" wide by 17½" long and two 5" wide by 30½" long for each shade. Cut 4"-wide strips of fusible interfacing by the length and center on the wrong side of each strip, keeping the ½" seam allowances free. Fold the strips in half, right sides together, and stitch along the long edge. Press the seams open and center in the back of each strip.

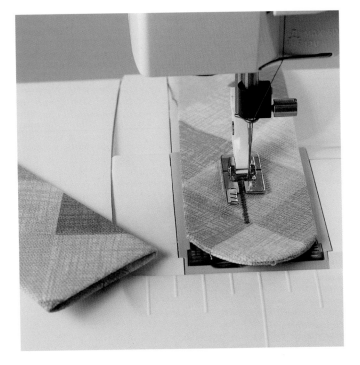

18 On the shorter straps, use a juice glass to trace a curved edge at one end. Stitch along the curved line. Trim close to the stitching and turn. On the long straps, stitch along one short edge. Clip the corners and turn. Press ½" to the inside on the unfinished edge of each strap. On the right side, stitch 2" buttonholes at the curved edge of the short straps.

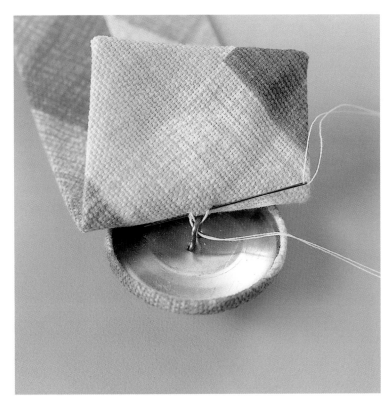

HANDY HINT

Buttonholes are usually placed ⁵/₈" from the edge of the garment or home decorating item. It is always best to stitch out a test buttonhole on scraps of the same fabric as the piece being sewn. Adjustment can then be made before finishing the project.

19 Cover the buttons according to the manufacturer's instructions. Stitch each button to the right side and in the center of the longer strap.

20 On the right side, measure 6" from each side edge and pin the short straps in place just under the stitching line for the casing. Baste. Turn the shade over and pin the long straps, seam sides to the lining, over the stitching line from the short straps. Stitch through all the layers.

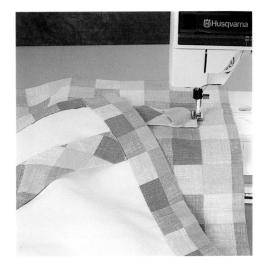

21 Insert a spring rod through the casing to hang the shade. Fold the shade up from the bottom and button in place at each strap to secure.

SHEER POCKETED SHOWER
CURTAIN

What fun to duplicate what you see in expensive catalogs for half

the cost by making it yourself! Learn to make patch pockets at the same time.

1 Cut one shower curtain 76" wide by 84" long. Cut four 7½" by the width of the fabric strips for pockets. Cut one 2" by 72" strip of interfacing.

2 Use a manila file folder to make a pressing template. Draw lines across the folder ½", 1", 2", 4" and 8" away from one edge.

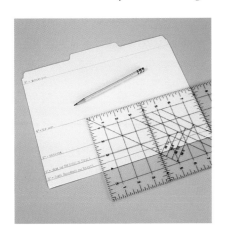

3 Use the pressing template to press an 8" hem on one 76" side. Open out the hem allowance and fold the cut edge in to the crease. Press the hem again to make a double-fold 4" hem. Pin the folded hem and topstitch close to the inner folded edge.

continued

DESIGN OPTIONS

*Use your pocket-enhanced shower curtain to communicate a theme
of bath-time fun. Make words from easy-to-sew letters. Then, add other found
objects, stitched colorful embroideries, or felt or craft foam shapes
to complete the look.*

4 Press a 2" hem on both 84" sides using the pressing
template. Open out the hem allowance and fold the
cut edge in to the crease. Refold the hem to make a
double-fold 1" hem. Pin the folded hem and topstitch close
to the inner folded edge.

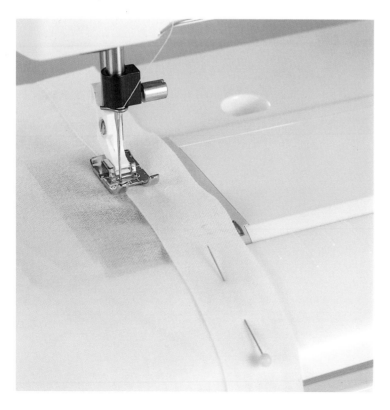

5 On the remaining side, use the
pressing template to press a 4"
hem for the top band. Open the hem
allowance and fold the cut edge in
to the crease. Place the long side of
the interfacing strip next to the
crease with the fusible side against
the hem allowance. Follow the
manufacturer's instructions for fusing
the interfacing.

7 Fold the hemmed shower curtain in half and crease. Starting 3" on either side of center, mark 12 vertical buttonholes approximately 6" apart across the top band. Sew vertical 1" buttonholes on the top band using your buttonhole sensor foot.

6 Open out the hem allowance and fold the cut edge in to the crease. Refold the hem to make a double-fold 2" hem. Pin the folded hem and topstitch close to the inner folded edge.

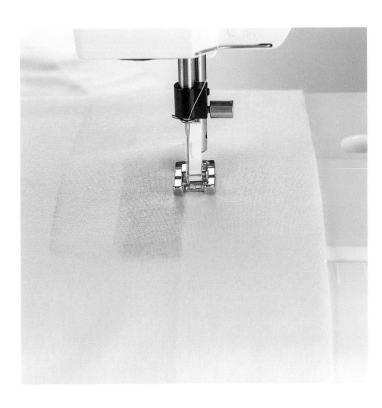

8 Using the pressing template, press a 1" hem on one long side of each pocket strip. Fold as above to make a double-fold ½" hem. Pin the folded hem and topstitch close to the inner folded edge.

continued

9 Cut the pocket strips into 48 - 7" pockets. Use the pressing template to press ½" seam allowances to the wrong side of each pocket on the remaining three sides.

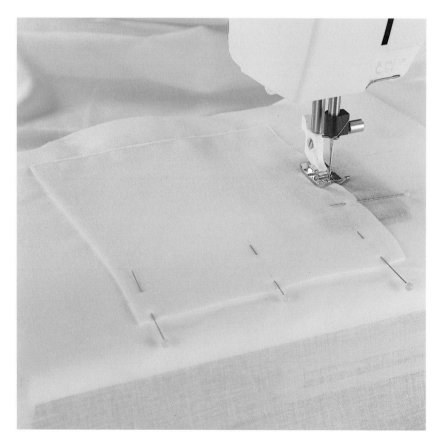

10 Pin a patch pocket 1" from either side of the center crease and 5" down from the top band. Pin a total of eight pockets 2" apart and 5" from the top band for the top row. Topstitch close to the edge of the pockets.

11 Pin the second row of pockets 3" below the first. Topstitch each pocket in place. Continue to pin and topstitch one row of pockets at a time until a total of six rows of pockets have been added.

12 For pocket inserts, lay the stencil backwards over the cut-away stabilizer. Use a marking pen to trace the outline of the letter.

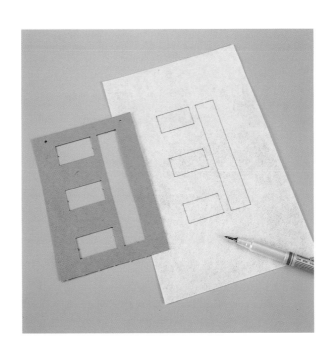

13 Layer the fabric, right side down, under two layers of stabilizer with the marked piece on top. Sew with a straight stitch following the outline. Trim away any fabric close to the stitching line.

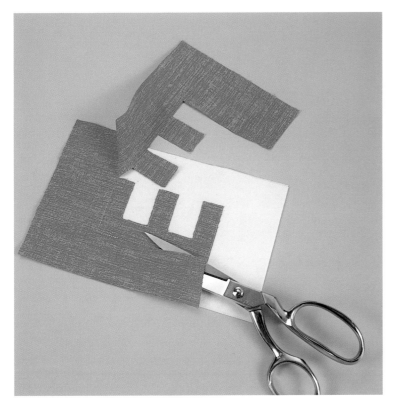

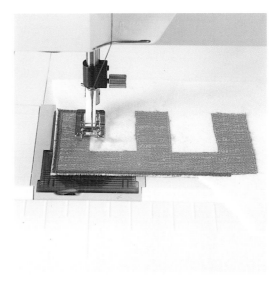

14 Using your decorative foot, with the fabric facing up, satin-stitch with rayon thread along the outside edge of each letter. Trim away the stabilizer close to the edge of the satin stitching.

BAG IT, COVER IT, OR MAT IT

Family Reunion
2000

CARRYALL CANVAS
TOTE BAG

This smart, tri-colored canvas tote can be used for just about anything. Perfect for carrying towels, lotions, magazines, and all the necessities to the beach, it's sturdy yet lightweight.

VOCABULARY

⁵⁄₈" seam allowance—standard allowance used for dressmaking.

Webbing—firmly woven band used for straps and belts.

TECHNIQUES YOU WILL LEARN

- Making box corners
- Sewing layers of canvas
- Stitching down webbing

Fabric: 1¹⁄₂ yards of natural-colored canvas (body)
1 yard of colored canvas (bottom and trim)
³⁄₄ yard of coordinating color of canvas (side bands)

Notions: 2¹⁄₄ yards of 1"-wide webbing
Ruler or tape measure
Matching sewing thread

Needles: Universal or denim needles #90/14 or larger (depending on the weight of the canvas)

1 From the natural-colored canvas, cut two rectangles, 16" by 23", for the body and one rectangle, 2" by 45", for the top band. From the 1 yard of canvas, cut two rectangles, 14" by 23", for the bag bottom and two, 1¹⁄₂" by 23", for trim. From the band canvas, cut two pieces, 6" by 23". Cut the webbing into two 40" lengths.

2 Press the 1¹⁄₂"-wide trim pieces in half lengthwise.

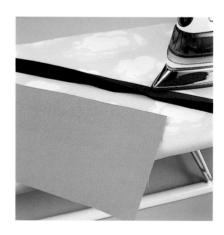

3 With raw edges together, pin the folded trim to the long edge of the side bands. Stitch the trim to the edge with a ⅝" seam allowance. Press the seam down toward the band.

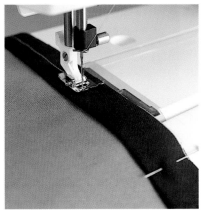

continued

4 From the right side, topstitch the
seam allowance down to hold.

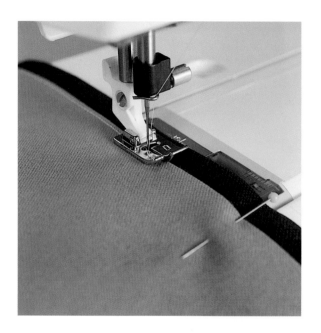

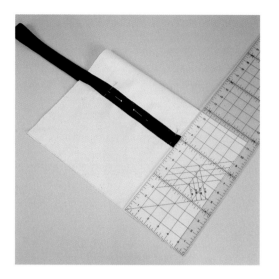

5 Mark the centers of each of the 23"-wide body
sections. Measure up 5" from the lower edges
and in 3½" from the center markings. Pin the
webbing along the markings and stitch in place.
Stop stitching 3" from the upper edge.

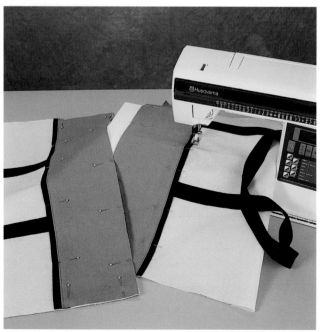

6 Layer the wrong side of
the trimmed bands over
the right side of the body
sections matching the bottom
edges and pin. Stitch the
trimmed band section to the
body panels along the trim
edge using your edgestitch or
blindhem foot. Baste the side
and bottom edges in place ½"
in from the edges.

7 Using a ⅝" seam allowance, stitch the lower basted edges of the body panels to one bottom section matching the raw edges. Press the seams down.

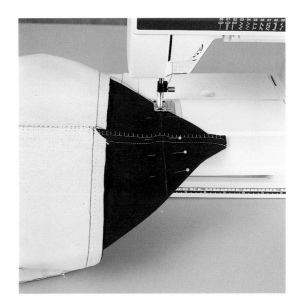

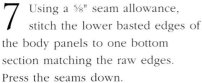

8 Fold the bag in half, right sides together, and match the top edges. Stitch the side seams from top to bottom with a ⅝" seam. Clean-finish the seam allowance edges with a 3-step zigzag.

9 Crease along the center of the bottom section. Bring the side seam to meet the crease, forming a triangle, and pin in place. Measure down and mark across the triangle at the point where the fabric is 6" from side to side. Stitch along the marking. Trim away the triangle fabric above the stitching.

10 Fold under ⅝" along both long edges of the remaining bottom lining piece. Fold the lining piece in half lengthwise and stitch ⅝" seams on both short ends.

11 Form the triangles as in Step 8. Stitch and trim the triangles.

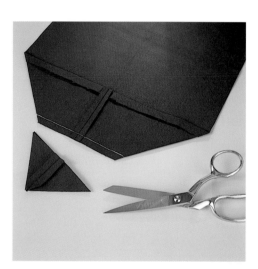

HANDY HINT

Most sewing machines today have what is called a "free-arm" sewing surface. This narrower working surface makes it easier to sew circular items.

12 With wrong sides together, pin the bottom lining inside the bottom of the bag matching the exposed stitching line with the fold top edge. Topstitch in place.

13 Fold under ½" on the remaining 2" by 45" band along one long and one short edge. Pin the band to the upper edge of the bag with the right side of the band to the wrong side of the bag. Stitch with a ⅝" seam. Trim the seam.

14 Fold the band over to the right side of the bag. Press and pin in place. Topstitch along the upper and lower edges of the band.

FLAP-TOP
SHOULDER BAG

Create this trendy color-coordinated canvas shoulder bag to match any outfit.

VOCABULARY

Grommets—metal rings attached to the fabric to reinforce eyelet holes.

TECHNIQUES
YOU WILL LEARN

- Sewing circles
- Sewing canvas
- Sewing webbing
- Attaching grommets

Fabric: ¹/₂ yard of two colors of canvas
  I yard of coordinating color of canvas
Notions: ³/₄ yard of webbing
  Matching sewing thread
  Fabric marking pen
Needles: Universal needles #90/12 or larger
  (depending on the weight of the canvas)
Other supplies: Grommets and grommet pliers

1 Cut two 9¼"-diameter circles from one ½ yard of canvas for the bottom and the lining. Cut three pieces from the same fabric, 3¼" by 26¾", for the band. From the other ½ yard of canvas, cut two rectangles, 9½" by 13" for the front flap. Cut one 1" by 26¾" strip from the same fabric for trim. Cut one rectangle, 11" by 26¾", from the coordinating canvas for the body.

2 Fold the 1" trim strip in half lengthwise and press.

3 Press under a ½" hem on the 3¼" by 26¾" band. Pin the pressed trim strip to the pressed hem on the band leaving ¼" of the trim exposed. Baste the trim in place.

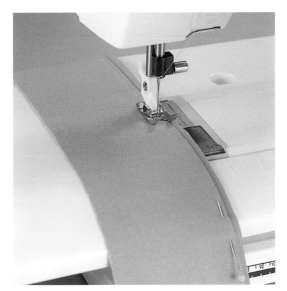

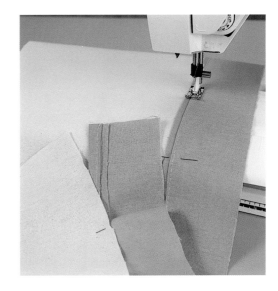

4 Pin the wrong side of the trimmed band to the right side along the lower edge of the body panel matching the edges. Edgestitch through all the layers.

continued

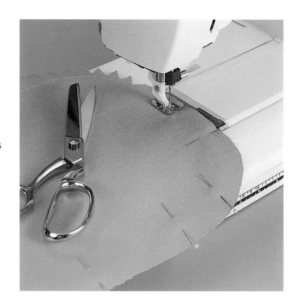

5 Stitch the back seam, matching the trim and the band edges. Clean-finish the seam allowance with a zigzag stitch to avoid raveling. Press the seam to one side.

6 Stitch the flap pieces together along three sides. Notch the corners, trim, turn, and press.

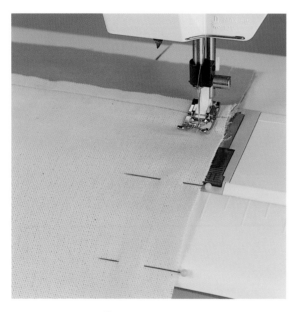

7 Edgestitch along all three sides using your edgestitch or blindhem foot. Fold the flap in half and mark the center. Set this piece aside.

HANDY HINT

To curve the corners on the flap, place a small plate at each corner and trace the edge.

HANDY HINT

Edgestitching will keep the under layer from rolling to the front. Use edgestitching on flaps, collars, cuffs, or any area where you want the layers held in place.

8 For the top band, stitch the upper edges together. Open the seam and press. Trim away about ¼" from the seam. Press under ½" on both long raw edges.

9 Stitch the back seam of the band. Open the seam, trim, and press. Notch the seam allowances.

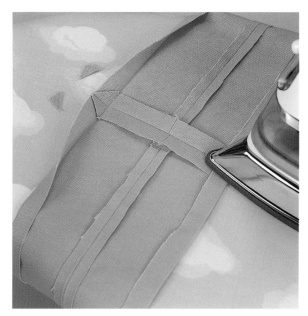

10 Pin the flap to the upper edge of the bag, matching the center mark on the flap with the back seam of the bag.

12 Baste the bottom bag pieces together along the outer edges.

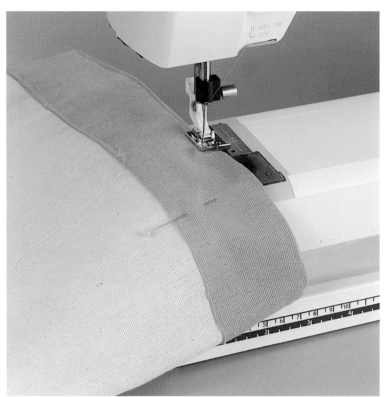

11 Place the band over the top edge of the bag, matching the seams and pin. Stitch along both the top and bottom edges of the band using your edgestitch or blindhem foot.

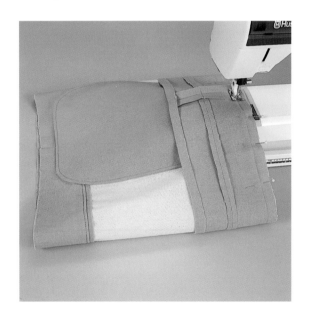

13 Baste ⅝" in along the lower edge of the bag band. Clip the seam allowance to the basting line.

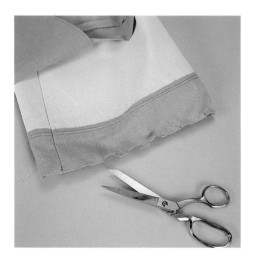

14 Fold the bottom piece of the bag in half and then again in quarters; mark. Quarter the bottom edge of the bag in the same way; mark. Pin the bottom piece to the bag piece, matching the markings.

15 Stitch using a ⅝" seam allowance. Trim the seam and overcast the edges with a zigzag or 3-step zigzag stitch.

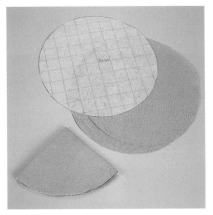

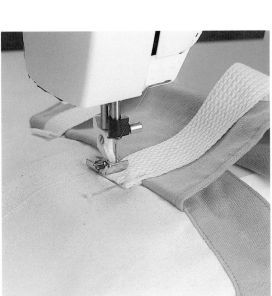

16 Fold under a ½" hem on the webbing. Measure 1½" in from the back seam and place the webbing at the flap seam. Stitch the webbing in place.

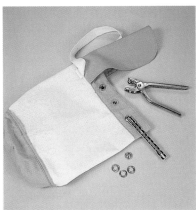

17 Measure and mark the placement of the grommets. Attach the grommets to the band, following the manufacturer's instructions.

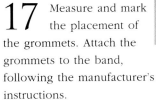

MEMORY
ALBUM COVER

Save all those precious photographs, ticket stubs, corsages, and other
memories from those special times in your life in a fabric-covered album you made yourself.

VOCABULARY

Photo transfer—method of transferring a photograph to fabric with heat or a copying machine.

TECHNIQUES YOU WILL LEARN

- Using decorative stitches
- Using photo transfers

Fabric: ¹/₂ yard of decorative fabric (Choose white or off-white 100% cotton if using a photo transfer process)

Notions: ¹/₂ yard of cotton batting
  Matching sewing thread
  Ruler or tape measure
  Ribbon, trims, buttons (optional)
  40 wt. rayon embroidery thread (optional)

Needles: Universal needles #80/12

Other supplies: 3-ring binder
  Photo transfer kit (optional)
  Favorite photos (optional)
  Permanent fabric marking pen (optional)

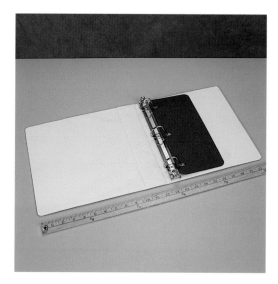

1 Open the flaps of the 3-ring binder to measure the length and width. Add 2" to the width and 9" to the length. Use these measurements to cut a rectangle from both the fabric and the batting. For ties, cut two 2" by 11½" rectangles from the fabric.

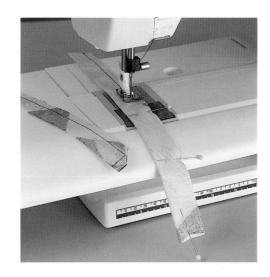

2 Make small clips along the long edges of the fabric rectangle 4½" from the corners. Find the center of the fabric piece by folding the long edges together and crease. On one short edge, press back 4½" to the wrong side of the fabric. Using the width measurement of the binder flap, divide by two, and mark that length on the lengthwise crease.

3 All seams are sewn with ½" seam allowances except where noted. Fold the ties in half lengthwise and, using the edge of the standard presser foot along the raw edge of the fabric, sew the long side and one short side. Trim the corner and turn right side out. Press. Repeat for the other tie.

continued

DESIGN OPTIONS

Follow the instructions packaged with the photo transfer paper to apply the photo to the fabric. Use decorative stitches from your sewing machine, or add ribbons or trim around the photo frame. Add names and dates with embroidery or a permanent fabric pen.

4 Lay the fabric right side up over the batting and pin.

5 Center the ties over both short sides, matching the raw edges. Starting at the corner, sew the short sides. Use the seamline as your guide to press the seam allowance to the inside of the cover. Topstitch the short edges with the presser foot along the folded edge of the fabric, or a ¼" seam allowance. Make sure the ties are folded away from the cover.

6 Fold the ties toward the right side of the cover and tack 3½" from the topstitched edge.

7 Fold the short sides at the clips with the right sides together to create the pockets. Sew the long edges. Trim the corner and half of the pocket seam allowance. Turn the pockets right side out.

8 Press the seam allowances of the long sides toward the inside of the cover. Topstitch the long sides with the presser foot along the folded edge of the fabric, or a ¼" seam allowance. Open the flaps of the 3-ring binder and insert them into the pockets of the cover.

KID'S
NAP MAT

Send your child or grandchild off to pre-school or kindergarten with this fold-up nap mat. Made out of color prints, your child will beg to take a nap!

VOCABULARY

Pin-baste—method of holding layers or fabric and batting together with pins spaced at close intervals.

TECHNIQUES YOU WILL LEARN

• Easy quilting

---

*Supplies are given for a finished mat 42" by 22".
Fabric: 1¹/₂ yards of decorator fabric for mat front
  1¹/₂ yards of coordinating fabric for mat back
  ³/₄ yard of coordinating fabric for pillow
Notions: 1¹/₂ yards of cotton batting
  4 yards coordinating jumbo covered cord with lip
  18" of Velcro® brand Soft & Flexible SEW-ON tape
  Fabric marking pen
  Matching sewing thread
Needles: Universal Needles #90/14
Other supplies: Rectangle pillow form 18" by 14"
  Yardstick

---

1 Cut two rectangles, 19" by 15", for the pillow front and back.

2 With right sides together, pin the pillow front to the back. Stitch using ½" seams, leaving an 8" opening for turning and stuffing. Cut across the corners to eliminate bulk and turn the pillow cover right side out. Press.

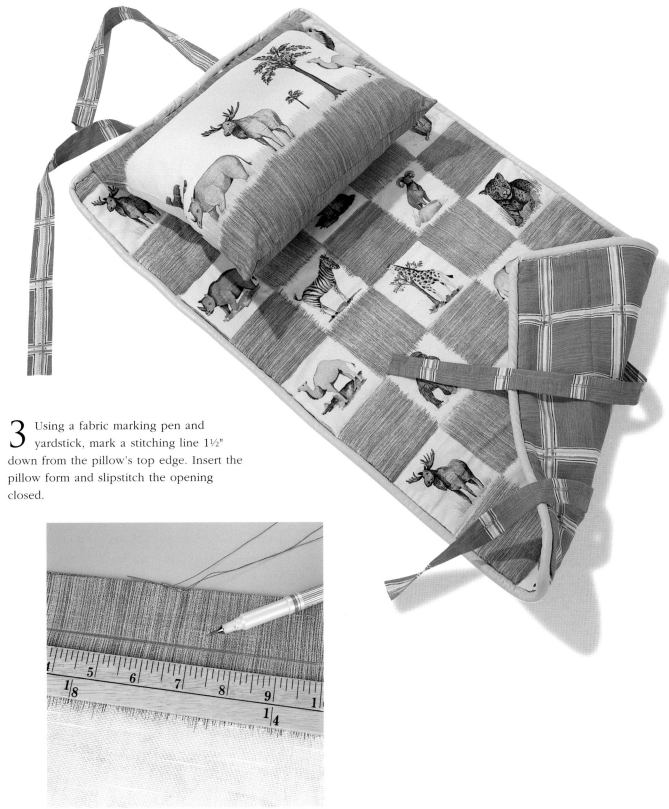

3 Using a fabric marking pen and
yardstick, mark a stitching line 1½"
down from the pillow's top edge. Insert the
pillow form and slipstitch the opening
closed.

continued

4 Push the pillow form down from the upper edge and pin along the marking. Carefully stitch along the marked line to create a flap.

HANDY HINT

If your machine is a tabletop model, support the pillow on the left of your machine with books or a box as you stitch.

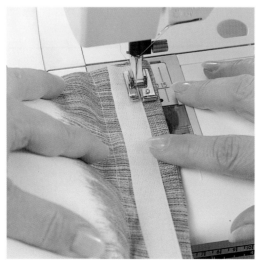

5 Center the hook side of Velcro® brand Soft & Flexible SEW-ON tape on the wrong side of the flap and stitch through all thicknesses along the outer edges of the tape. Set the pillow aside.

6 Cut front and back sections for the mat 43" by 23". Cut the batting 43" by 23". Cut four ties 24" by 3" from the mat backing fabric.

7 To make the ties, turn under the cut edge on one short end; press. Fold the fabric strips lengthwise in thirds overlapping the edges slightly; press. Using the flatlock stitch on your machine, stitch down the center of the tie incorporating the cut edge into the stitching. Trim any raw edges, if needed.

8 Place two ties at the upper edge on the mat backing section 6" in from each long edge. Baste. Using a fabric marker and ruler, measure 12" up from the short end and 6" in from the long edge; mark the fabric. Pin the remaining two ties at the markings. Stitch all ties in place to secure.

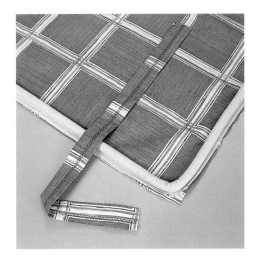

9 Pin the covered cord to the right side of the mat backing having the cut edges even with the cording lip and the cord facing inside of the mat. Using a zipper foot positioned on the right side of the needle, baste the cording to the pillow. As you approach each corner, cut the cord lip into the corner and at each side of the corner to ease the cord around the edge. At the end, remove 1" of stitching from each end of the cording. Trim the filler cord so the ends just meet. Fold under ½" of the cording fabric and wrap it around the end. Continue stitching joining the ends.

10 Lay the batting on the wrong side of the mat front section. Pin-baste the layers together in the center and at 1" intervals to hold in place.

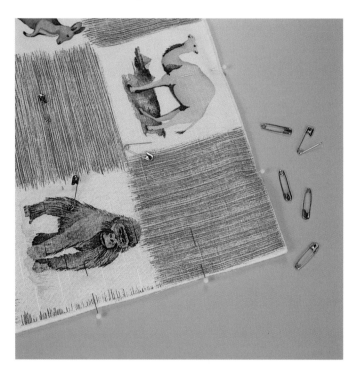

11 Pin the remaining side of hook-and-loop tape on the right side of the mat front through all layers 1" from the upper edge. Stitch in place along the outer edges of the tape.

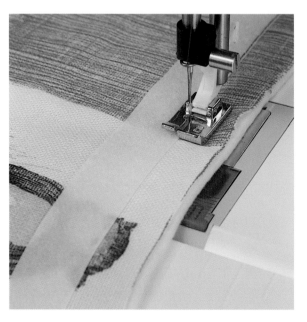

12 Place the mat backing on top of the front, right sides together; pin. Stitch around the edges with a zipperfoot and adjusted needle position, leaving a 12" opening at the lower edge for turning. Trim the batting 1/8" from the seam; trim the corners diagonally.

HANDY HINT

Use safety pins to hold all the batting and fabric layers together. Begin in the center of the mat, then pin the edges. Be sure the pins are within the stitching lines.

13 Turn the mat right side out and press lightly. Press under the seam allowance along the open edge and machine-stitch close to the pressed edge to finish.

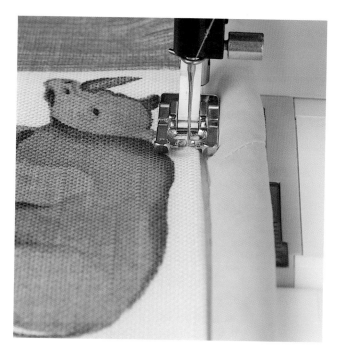

14 Carefully pin-baste all the layers together. Quilt the mat along the design vertical and horizontal lines to outline and define it and keep the layers from shifting too much.

HANDY HINT

If your fabric does not have distinct vertical and horizontal lines, you can quilt diagonally. Mark quilting lines parallel to each other with a yardstick and use as a stitching guide. Most machines come with a quilting guide to help you keep the lines of stitching straight. See your instruction manual for details.

HANDY HINT

A dual-feed foot is a useful attachment when quilting. The action of the foot will prevent puckering and shifting of the fabric layers.

15 Attach the pillow to the mat aligning the hook-and-loop tape. To store, wrap the mat around the pillow and secure with the ties.

Summer Beach

BLANKET

Make this durable and versatile beach mat for yourself. The fabric used for this project won't fade or rot from exposure to the sun.

VOCABULARY

Binding—strips of fabric used to encase raw edges or seams; often referred to as bias binding, binding can be cut on the straight-of-grain.

TECHNIQUES YOU WILL LEARN

- Making straight binding
- Edgestitching
- Making straps

FABRIC: 2 yards of 54"-wide Sunbrella™ canvas
2 yards of contrasting canvas for binding
NOTIONS: Fabric marking pen
Matching sewing thread
Ruler or tape measure
NEEDLES: Jeans or Universal needles #90/14

HANDY HINT

The binding strips can be cut on the straight grain for this project since they are applied to straight edges. For more flexible binding, cut the strips on the bias grain. Bias strips are useful when binding curved edges as the fabric will stretch with the curve.

1 Straighten and cut the canvas 72" by 54". For the binding, cut two 2½"-wide strips of contrasting fabric the finished length plus 4" for turning at the corners and two 2½"-wide strips the finished width plus 4".

2 Cut two ties 40" long by 2½" wide from the contrasting fabric. For the strap, cut one 36" long by 2½"-wide piece from the contrasting fabric.

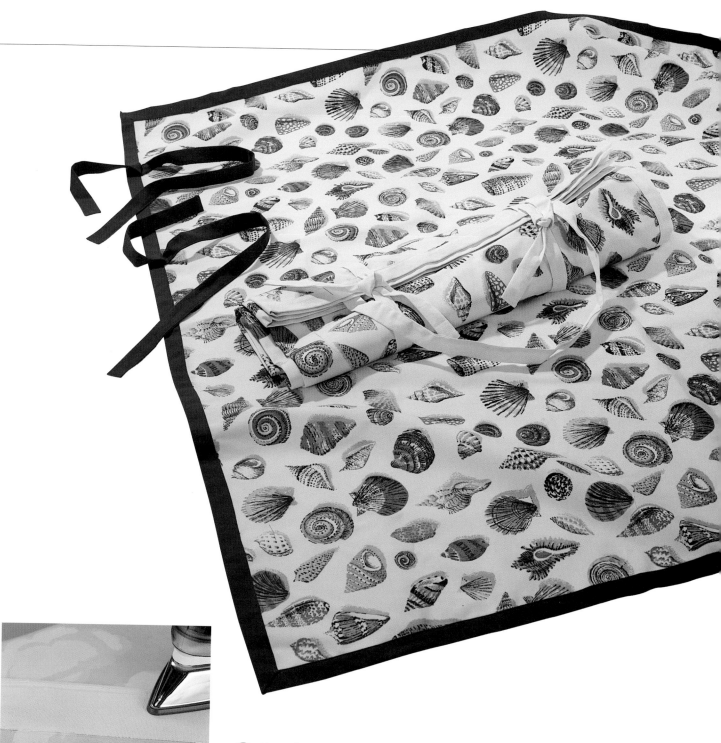

3 To make the ties, press under ½"
along all the edges. Press under ½"
along the long edges of the strap. Fold the
ties and the strap in half lengthwise,
press, and pin.

continued

4 Edgestitch the ties using your blindhem or edgestitch foot to guide you. Move the needle position as necessary.

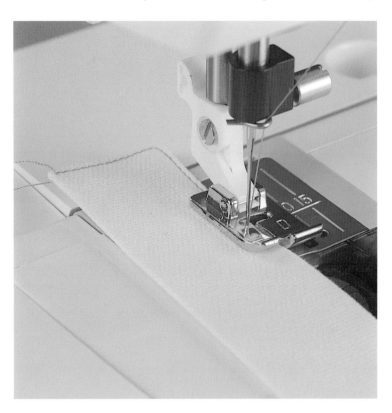

5 Fold the ties down from one end 13".

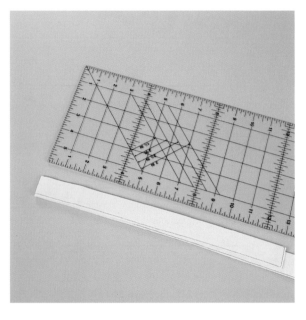

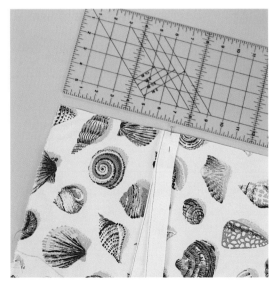

6 For the tie placement, mark using a fabric marking pen on the right side of the fabric 7" from one edge at the upper end of the mat. Measure over 20" from the edge for the second tie and mark. Place the folded ends of the ties at the marks. Machine-baste the ties in place.

7 For the strap placement, measure and mark on the right side of the fabric at the opposite end of the mat, 6" and 21" from the edge. Machine-baste the cut ends of the straps at the markings.

8 To bind the mat, wrap the binding around the cut edges and pin. Edgestitch close to the edge being careful to catch the binding on the under side. Fold under the ends at each corner and stitch.

9 To carry and store, fold the mat in half lengthwise with wrong sides together. Then, fold up the ends and tie around the roll. Carry with the strap.

GLOSSARY OF TERMS

As with any area of expertise, there are terms used relative only to that field. We have tried to list as many terms or techniques that you may encounter as you begin your journey into sewing.

Air-soluble—marks that disappear after time in the air

Appliqué—method of applying fabric pieces on top of a base fabric with a satin-stitch edging

Backstitch—to take a few stitches backward at the beginning and end of a seam to prevent the seam from opening

Bartack—very narrow, dense line of zigzag stitching used to hold layers in place

Baste—to take long stitches either by machine or by hand to hold the pieces together temporarily before sewing the final seam

Batting—filling used as stuffing; can be made from cotton, wool, fiberfil, silk, or other materials

Bias—diagonal of fabric, true bias is 45 degrees to the grain

Bias tape—bias-cut fabric which can be purchased or made; most often used to encase edges

Binding—strips of fabric used to encase raw edges or seams; often referred to as bias binding; binding can be cut on the straight-of-grain for straight edges

Blindhem—hem sewn with invisible stitches either by hand or machine

Boxed pillow—additional banding added between pillow top and bottom forming a boxed shape; pillows can be round, square, rectangular or other unique shapes (e.g. stars, triangles, etc.)

Brush fringe—ornamental trim with loose strands of thread, yarn, or beads attached to a woven band

Café Curtain—used most often on double-hung windows, a short curtain the length of which is slightly greater than the window split

Casing—a stitched channel used on simple curtains or valances to hold the curtain rod; also used for waistbands or on sleeves to hold elastic band

Casing with header—stitched channel with extra fabric above; used on café curtains, valances, and along casings where added fabric interest is needed

Chair tie—tassels linked by straight length (approximately 27") of twisted cord

Channel quilting—to stitch with parallel straight lines through all layers of fabric and batting creating a quilted effect

Clean-finish—to overcast the edges of the seam allowance with a zigzag, 3-step zigzag, overcasting stitches, or with the serger to prevent raveling

Clip—to cut into the seam allowance around curves and at corners

Cluny lace—a coarse bobbin lace either made by hand or machine

Covered cord—often referred to as piping, fabric-covered cord is used as trim on pillows, cushions, and upholstered pieces as well as on the edge of collars, cuffs, or other garments; filler cable cord is wrapped with a bias strip of fabric leaving a narrow edge of fabric to be stitched into the seam allowance

Crazy patch—to piece a variety of fabric types and shapes together; embroidery is often used as topical embellishment

Cutting line—marked line on which to cut out fabric

Double-fold hem—to fold up the edge of the fabric twice by the same amount; hem can be finished with a blindhem or edgestitched

Drop length—the amount of fabric that hangs over the edge of a tabletop

Edgestitch—to stitch very close to the finished or folded edge as on hems, collars, or cuffs

Facing—a piece of fabric applied to another to finish the edge instead of a binding

Finger-press—gently crease fabric with pressure from your fingers

Flange—a wide flat band often used on the edge of pillows

Fuse—to adhere interfacing or fleece to a fabric generally by heat from an iron and pressure. It is best to follow the manufacturer's directions for each fusing product.

Grain—direction in which the threads are woven; lengthwise grain runs parallel to the selvedge; crosswise grain runs from selvedge to selvedge; there is usually a small amount of stretch to the crosswise grain

Grommets—metal rings attached to the fabric to reinforce eyelet holes

Gusset—piece of fabric inserted at sides for wider opening

Interfacing—additional fabric applied for stability and shape inside a project

Lining—fabric used on the reverse side to provide stability to a project; the lining can often be seen so the same fabric or an equally as nice fabric is used for lining

Marking—to transfer symbols from pattern to fabric for construction

Miter—to form a square corner by stitching the fabrics on a diagonal

Nap—a finishing technique applied to fabric where the fibers lie flat in one direction

Needle positions—the ability to move the needle of the sewing machine off-center in increments to the right or left

Notch—to cut small triangles of fabric from the seam allowance on concave curves to allow the seam to lie flat

Notions—those items other than the fabric needed for the project

Overlay—piece of fabric or lace placed on top of another for decorative purposes

Patch pockets—pocket that is stitched on the outside of the garment or item; may have a flap

Patchwork—also called piecing, sewing a variety of smaller pieces of fabric together to form a larger piece. In traditional piecing for quilt making, the pieces are usually sewn together with a $1/4$" seam allowance

Pattern tracing paper—fabric-type material or paper used for pattern making; usually grided with 1" squares

Photo transfer—method of transferring a photograph to fabric with heat or a copying machine

Pin-baste—method of holding layers of fabric and batting together with pins spaced at close intervals

Pinking—to cut the edges with a pinking shears (zigzag cut edge)

Piping—covered cord, twisted cord, or edging treatment used on pillows, cushions, upholstery, or clothing; can be filled or unfilled

Pivot—to leave the needle in the fabric, raise the presser foot and turn the fabric before continuing to stitch

Pre-shrink—to treat fabric before sewing by washing or dry cleaning to prevent additional shrinking

Press—to apply pressure to fabric making or setting creases or opening seam allowances using a temperature-controlled iron

Pressing template—ruled template used as a guide for pressing up hems, turning in seam allowances, or for exact edges

Raw edge—unfinished cut or torn edge of the fabric

Return—section of curtain or valance from corner of rod to wall

Roman shade—flat fabric attached to window at the top; fabric is drawn up from the bottom with ring tape

Satin stitch—very close zigzag stitches used on appliqués, to fill areas of embroidery, or along the edges of fabric

Seam allowance—the remaining fabric left after a seam is sewn; a $5/8$" seam allowance is typical for garment sewing; a $1/2$" seam allowance is typical for home decorating

Seam sealant—liquid notion that secures seams and threads, and prevents fraying on edges

Selvedge—may also be spelled selvage, a tightly woven band on the lengthwise edge of the fabric

Shaped valance—valance with curved edge; can be formal or informal depending on the fabric

Slipstitch—simple hand stitch used to close an opening with small invisible stitches

Stabilizer—term used to describe any backing material used to reinforce an area while stitching; term most often used for appliqué, embroidery, or other decorative work; often torn away after technique is completed

Staystitch—a reinforcing stitch usually stitched $^1/_8$" inside the seamline to control stretching on curves and in corners

"Stitch-in-the-ditch"—method of stitching in the groove of the seam through all thicknesses to hold the under layer in place

Sunbrella® fabric—brand of fabric that will not fade or deteriorate from the sun; mildew resistant

Tabs—loops of fabric used as a method for hanging on curtain rods and dowels, or for threading cord; can be used for button closures or belts

Tension—the equal pull on the upper and bobbin threads on the sewing machine

Topstitch—pronounced stitching usually done with a heavier thread close to a seam or finished edge

Trim—to cut away excess fabric from the seam allowance, corners, or curves for easier turning and pressing; also decorative edging

Turn—to reverse the sides of the fabric such as "turn to the right side"

Twisted cord—decorative trim used on edges of pillows, cushions, upholstery, and clothing. Decorative threads are wrapped together forming cord with or without a lip attached

Valance—a topper for full-length curtains or drapes or used to visually connect short curtains that only cover part of the window; usually 10"-16" in length

Velvet board—board covered with pin points used for pressing napped fabrics

Water-soluble—marks that disappear with water application

Webbing—firmly woven band used for straps and belts

Welt seam—type of seam with one seam allowance trimmed; both allowances pressed to one side and topstitched

ACKNOWLEDGMENTS

We gratefully acknowledge the following companies for their support and the contribution of their products toward the production of this book. We hope you continue to support these companies by purchasing their products at your local sewing store and Keep the World Sewing!

Fabrics

Dan River Inc.
1325 Ave. of the Americas
New York, NY 10019

Waverly
79 Madison Ave.
New York, NY 10016

Threads and Notions

Coats & Clark
Two LakePointe Plaza
4135 South Stream Blvd.
Charlotte, NC 28217

Prym Drtiz Corporation
P.O. Box 5028
Spartenburg, SC 29304

Trims

Conso
P.O. Box 326
513 N. Duncan By-Pass
Union, SC 29379

Hirschberg Schutz
650 Liberty Ave.
Union, NJ 07083

Batting

Quilters Dream Batting
2700 Avenger Dr. #109
Virginia Beach, VA 23452

Pillow Forms

Fairfield Processing Co.
P.O. Box 1130
Danbury, CT 06810

Interfacing

Freudenberg Nonwovens
3440 Industrial Dr.
Durham, NC 27704

INDEX

METRIC EQUIVALENTS

Inches to Millimeters and Centimeters
MM - millimeters   CM - centimeters

Inches	MM	CM	Inches	CM	Inches	CM
1/8	3	0.3	9	22.9	30	76.2
1/4	6	0.6	10	25.4	31	78.7
3/8	10	1.0	11	27.9	32	81.3
1/2	13	1.3	12	30.5	33	83.8
5/8	16	1.6	13	33.0	34	86.4
3/4	19	1.9	14	35.6	35	88.9
7/8	22	2.2	15	38.1	36	91.4
1	25	2.5	16	40.6	37	94.0
1 1/4	32	3.2	17	43.2	38	96.5
1 1/2	38	3.8	18	45.7	39	99.1
1 3/4	44	4.4	19	48.3	40	101.6
2	51	5.1	20	50.8	41	104.1
2 1/2	64	6.4	21	53.3	42	106.7
3	76	7.6	22	55.9	43	109.2
3 1/2	89	8.9	23	58.4	44	111.8
4	102	10.2	24	61.0	45	114.3
4 1/2	114	11.4	25	63.5	46	116.8
5	127	12.7	26	66.0	47	119.4
6	152	15.2	27	68.6	48	121.9
7	178	17.8	28	71.1	49	124.5
8	203	20.3	29	73.7	50	127.0

METRIC CONVERSION CHART

Yards	Inches	Meters	Yards	Inches	Meters
1/8	4.5	0.11	1 1/8	40.5	1.03
1/4	9	0.23	1 1/4	45	1.14
3/8	13.5	0.34	1 3/8	49.5	1.26
1/2	18	0.46	1 1/2	54	1.37
5/8	22.5	0.57	1 5/8	58.5	1.49
3/4	27	0.69	1 3/4	63	1.60
7/8	31.5	0.80	1 7/8	67.5	1.71
1	36	0.91	2	72	1.83